A TEENAGE GUIDE
TO AN ADULT WORLD

GEOFF STUART

BALBOA.PRESS
A DIVISION OF HAY HOUSE

Balboa Press books may be ordered through booksellers or by contacting:

Balboa Press
A Division of Hay House
1663 Liberty Drive
Bloomington, IN 47403
www.balboapress.com.au
AU TFN: 1 800 844 925 (Toll Free inside Australia)
AU Local: (02) 8310 7086 (+61 2 8310 7086 from outside Australia)

Because of the dynamic nature of the Internet, any web addresses or links contained in this book may have changed since publication and may no longer be valid. The views expressed in this work are solely those of the author and do not necessarily reflect the views of the publisher, and the publisher hereby disclaims any responsibility for them.

The author of this book does not dispense medical advice or prescribe the use of any technique as a form of treatment for physical, emotional, or medical problems without the advice of a physician, either directly or indirectly. The intent of the author is only to offer information of a general nature to help you in your quest for emotional and spiritual well-being. In the event you use any of the information in this book for yourself, which is your constitutional right, the author and the publisher assume no responsibility for your actions.

Any people depicted in stock imagery provided by Getty Images are models, and such images are being used for illustrative purposes only. Certain stock imagery © Getty Images.

Print information available on the last page.

ISBN: 979-8-7652-0002-5 (sc)
ISBN: 979-8-7652-0001-8 (e)

Library of Congress Control Number: 2024914290

Balboa Press rev. date: 07/17/2024

You grow old as a child only to become young as an adult – the most exciting stage of your life. Now, let your life as an adult begin.

INSPIRATIONS – can a few words of wisdom change your view of the world?

"There are plenty of screws loose in my head, and I am a super idealist"

Alfred Nobel (1833-1896)
   – The inventor of dynamite.
It was his bequest that enabled the 'Nobel Prize' for peace to be established.

"Sometimes in life, you just have to ignore the red lights"
Singer/songwriter, Kev Carmody.

"Do the things you hate first, then your head and day are clear to do the things you like and enjoy"

HAPPINESS comes from having something bigger than our self to care about.

Enthusiasm is not a substitute for motivation.

Arrogance and ignorance often go hand in hand.

For every 'no' you receive, the closer you are to a 'yes'.

The road to success starts with a single step, BUT make sure that step is in the right direction

Not all advice is good advice. Remember… professionals built the unsinkable 'Titanic'!

The greatest luxury in the world is having a passport to travel.

Life is like a magnet. It draws you to the things you like and pushes you away from the things you don't like!

It is not what you make (earn from working), it is what you keep. Money saved is money earned.

To buy or not to buy- It's an equation, a balancing act. Is what you are about to purchase of greater or lesser value to you than the money you are about to spend?

Choose your friends wisely. If you associate with fools, you too will be a fool.

It's easier to drop a friend than keep them if they are taking you in a direction you don't want to go.

We write our own story of life, one day and one night at a time.

The reason for a coach is to push you to achieve more than you thought you could.

A great boss can be a teacher to empower you. You can also learn from a bad boss too. In life you may well encounter both.

Whenever you see a problem – Look for the opportunity.

"Technology changes, but people stay the same".
(Andrew Chen, Uber)

If we don't learn from our mistakes, we will continue to make them in the future.

We use street lights to guide our pathway in the night. We use our brain to guide us in our life.

"Sometimes the greatest walls we face are the ones that we place in front of ourselves". Boy George

"Not only does God play dice but…he sometimes throws the dice where they can't be seen." Professor Stephen Hawking (1942-2018)

"Love is the poetry of the senses" Honoré Balzac

GETTING TO KNOW 'YOU'

At 18 you have already enjoyed the first chapters of your life, but there are so many more exciting chapters and stories to be told.

Maybe think of your life as a journey from 0 to 100. You start at zero and then it is a question of how far up the scale of achievement and success you achieve during your life journey. Your life is and will be uniquely yours.

There will of course be good times and bad times, many rough patches, laughter and sad times as well as time to reflect, but hopefully you will find a few clues, some guideposts, ideas, thoughts and ideas in this book that will help you find your way.

Life is a story – and your life will also become *that* story.

INTRODUCTION

I'M NOT a psychologist, a medico, psychotherapist, lawyer, social worker, youth advisor, councilor, monk, rabbi, guru, archbishop or even one of the three wise men! I am simply a person.

Sure, I've been to school and even university, worked a lot in all sorts of jobs – some good, some bad, traveled quite a lot, stayed home, slept in and woken up early and woken up late too. I have also met lots of people – good, bad, young, old and had my good times and my share of bad times too.

There are things that I am proud of, and things that I am not. I have mixed with some very rich people and some very poor people and met a lot of people who are somewhere in between. I have also been cheated, robbed, crashed a car, been sick, smoked, not smoked, been drunk, sober, seen the effect of drugs, almost drowned and the list goes on.

I have also been alone and shared a bed, played sport and done nothing at all. I have been in love, fallen out of love, hated a few people, been sad, sick, seen people cry, people die, babies born, been in a war zone and I've spent a lot of time being happy.

As you might suspect, I have also done a lot of research into life and the way that people develop their lives, their careers, fall in love and out of love and have success but also failure.

What I have found is that whatever people put into life is very much what they get out of it. But there is a lot of luck involved in life too. Life never runs in a straight line.

People can sit on the sidelines, or get involved, and almost universally people want to feel good, have food to eat, a safe place to live, work and have family and friends whose company they enjoy.

That all sounds pretty simple, doesn't it, yet the world is a complex place, and you only need to listen to one news broadcast to realize how many people in the world are facing their own hardships, successes and also failures.

In your life you will have good times and bad times. You will have a lot of good times, but you will also have bad times too. It is impossible to avoid them both.

When you are 18 however, there is a whole world waiting for you. You are about to embark on one of the most exciting times in your life.

While I cannot stop you making mistakes in your life, it may make a difference if you know a little more about what to expect out of life, and how you can plan your life better.

In one sense, this book is a guide, and in another, it is a book of discovery. It is about life.

It is also a book written for you – not your parents, grandparents or the kids next door. It is written for you.

Maybe you will learn lots, or maybe learn absolutely nothing at all.

Whether you read it or not, I cannot force you. It is your decision.

Life is exactly like that, a question of choice. It is your choice. Not mine. It really is up to you!

However, I would like to ask you a favor.

If you like the book, or maybe hate it, pass it on to someone who you think will either love it or hate it too!

I believe that books should never be simply stuck on a bookshelf – be that bookshelf real or as an e-book.

You can sell the book, give it away or email it to a friend. I really don't mind and of course, you can also trash it!

At the end of the book write or add some of your own thoughts, your name, or email address with even some drawings, or anything else that takes your fancy. You can also write absolutely nothing at all if that is what you want to do.

Maybe what you write may help someone else, and maybe it won't help.

It will however make this book very special, because it will carry your thoughts on to anyone else who reads the book after you.

The worst thing that you can do is place this book on a bookshelf or not download it onto your computer, tablet or smart phone.

Go for it. Have fun in whatever you do.

Remember, time has a way of escaping from all of us.

Author – Geoff Stuart

LEARNING -

At school, the two most important subjects are English (if it is your first language) and Mathematics. One involves words and the other numbers. Like them or loathe them, you need to use both words and numbers as a central part in your life.

WORDS

You can chase them, fight them, play with them, toy with them, even get upset by them, but ultimately you will use them to create, build, influence people and challenge what is, what could be, and what will happen to you and the world around you.

How then will you use this gift?

NUMBERS

There is no way to avoid them. While most people think in words and express themselves through words, there are also people who think almost purely in numbers. Numbers tell a story. They are the 'black and white' reality of life – the facts that tell a story.

We use numbers to count and record money, to measure wealth, value, distance, to add, subtract, multiply and divide to create new numbers and those numbers will in turn tell a story.

Think of numbers as the dollars in your pocket.

How will you make numbers work for you?
How will you make words work for you?

CONTENTS

CHAPTER ONE
LIFE – THE BIG PICTURE

Age is an attitude – Never tell yourself that you are either too young or too old – you are just the age that you are for one short, single year.

It is funny isn't it! You arrive on the planet as a great bundle of joy and then immediately begin to cry your eyes out!

Even if you don't cry, someone will give you a great whack on your 'not so pretty end' to jumpstart your life. There's no escape. You're going to enjoy life, whether you like it or not!

Welcome to life on earth!

Fortunately or not fortunately you had absolutely no choice about what you looked like, if you were born as a boy or a girl, and how, where and why you landed on earth and you had absolutely no choice about who your parents would be.

Your parents probably 'oohed' and 'aahed' over you and invited the relatives over to see how 'cute you were' even if you were as bald as a badger or looked like a bear rug. There you were all crinkled and wrinkled, but 'ever so cute', all wrapped in your baby boy blue, baby girl pink, or maybe even yellow if they weren't too sure!

Nonetheless, there you were, the 'new baby', and your parents were in shock! You were beautiful though! Absolutely no doubt!

Trouble was the only thing your parents knew about babies was what they saw on a video and learnt from friends, their mother or in baby class. They had learnt all about breathing properly as you got ready to shoot through the door, and to always stay calm! Well that was the theory, but now you were real!

The real thing, living, breathing, and crying, but not necessarily in that order!

Your dad and mum were now parents. Responsible adults! Possibly D.I.N.K.S (Double income no kids) no more! They could only look back to the time when they themselves were kids!

They were really grownups now! There was no escape. You were not going back, and they would have to learn fast to understand everything about you. Everything from top to bottom! You were now the centre of attraction- the main event, and if you had older sisters or brothers, you were, at least as the new baby, still the main attraction.

In a certain sense you were probably a bit of an experiment, an adventure into the unknown, but very quickly they would have to adjust everything in their life.

So, how is your life going so far?

You are growing up fast and have probably left school already. School was your life. It is where your friends were. There were kids you liked and kids you didn't. Probably you enjoyed some subjects, and maybe disliked others. You possibly preferred playing video games and messaging on Facebook to studying, and you probably knew all the latest groups and watched their Utube videos. If you're a girl, you're checking out boys, and vice versa, and you're worried about the way you look and what your friends think of you.

Probably you are also worried about what lies ahead with your life and maybe wondering what will happen in your own life – what you will be doing this year and the years ahead.

Will you be working, and if so where? Will you have finished studying? Will you still be playing sport? Who will you be friends with? Will you have children yourself, be married or single or just recently divorced? Where will you be living? Who will your friends be?

Do I know? Do your friends know, and what about your parents? Do they know? Even if you think you know yourself, you are probably wrong!

So, what is this book about?

Well it's about *you,* and a whole lot of things that will hopefully help you understand *who you are* and what *you need to do* to understand the world you're about to enter - the world of adults.

The book is not very long, and the chapters are short, which hopefully makes it easier to read. Some things you may believe, and others not, but that's OK. Not everything you hear in life will be true, and you have every right to question, analyze, and make your own judgment about what's right, wrong or halfway in between! After all you are starting to become *the boss* in charge of your life, and if you make the most of your life, or even stuff it up, you're still *the boss*- the one in charge! No one to answer to but yourself!

So, if you are going to be *the boss*, the *'Numero Uno'*, the one in charge - then the more you know about life, the more you will get from life. It may be a bit scary, but it is also exciting too. Your life as an adult is about to begin!

CHAPTER TWO
THE CERTAINTY OF LIFE

To walk, run or take the roller coaster...

"Changing everything is a delightful opportunity"
'Client Earth' Lawyer – James Thornton

Every day when you wake up, you have a choice. You can stay in bed, get up, go out, or just lounge about watching TV, or do something entirely different.

You may go to college, or work, visit friends, go shopping, catch a bus, study, play sport, or do any of a thousand different things. Life is made up of thousands of small insignificant decisions every day, yet some of these will be crucial to how your life evolves, and others will just blend together into a general blur of activity.

They say that there is only one thing certain in life, and that is apart from taxes, that having been born, you will also eventually die! Sad that really! Rich, poor, beggar, thief... no matter who you are; what you do; how clever you are; how much money you have or how little; the certainty of life is in fact death, at least to your life on Earth.

Yet, for all that certainty, the other reality is that no two lives will exactly mirror another. We all enter this life with a different personality, a different view of the world, and we will all experience the world and what it offers in very different ways. Given the huge number of people who live on this planet, this is truly remarkable.

Every person will have a different personality and each will experience life in a different way. That includes you!

Your life will not be the same as your parents, and it won't be the same as your brothers and sisters, or even your friends - it will be unique to just you.

Given all the world's technology and the vast experience that has been built up over thousands of years, it is amazing that none of us know with any certainty where our lives will take us.

Sure, we can guess at what will happen and we all hope to live a long, happy and prosperous life, but will your life turn out the way you planned, the way you hoped, or take you on a completely different direction. No one can tell you and you don't know yourself. Only time will tell.

Time itself is a funny concept. While some people rush through life, with no time to spare, and none to waste, others see that there's lots of time, so why rush?

For Hindus they liken life to that of a flower. A flower begins life as a seed blown by the wind, which comes to Earth to live. It may fall on fertile soil, or a rock, or be washed down a river, but when it finds the right surrounds it will grow first as a seedling, to become a small plant, until all its beauty is revealed as a flower. The plant may flower once or many times, but in time the flower's color will fade, the plant's strength will wilt and the plant will eventually die, leaving its seeds to regenerate as new plants.

A human life is much the same! It may last just a few short minutes or more than a hundred years. It will grow and develop and flower as youth becomes adult, and then slowly, ever so slowly it will fade into eventual old age and death.

Buddhists believe that life is made up of cycles, with each cycle lasting twelve years. So, if you live to the age of 36, you will have lived through three cycles, while if you lived to 96, then you would have lived through eight life cycles.

Christians too have their view of life on earth and an afterlife, with the Christian religion based on the Bible and its teachings, with the promise of an afterlife in heaven or hell, based on how your life on earth was lived.

The Islamic religion is based on worship of Allah (God), with Muslims believing that the life on earth is only a transition that precedes the eternal life.

All religions lay down the principles of how to live a good life, looking after your own life, respecting others, and giving reverence to God.

So, who is correct, or is it simply a matter of an unanswered puzzle?

With no certain answer, you will have to make up your own mind, and whether you study religion or ignore it, you will ultimately decide on a set of values to govern your life and develop an unspoken code of conduct for yourself to live by.

It does seem however that childhood is an incredibly special time in people's lives. If you talk with very old people, you will find that they often relate more to their childhood than to any other part of their life. They may ignore their career, and many other aspects of their adult life, linking emotionally far closer to their own childhood.

Adults too, in times of high stress will often relate the immediate crisis to a situation in their childhood, when they experienced a similarly stressful situation. The hurt in a childhood can last a lifetime!

As much as you did or did not have control, hopefully you had a happy childhood.

To create happiness, may or may not be easy, but it certainly means doing more of the things you enjoy than the things you don't. For some people, this may be easy, for others it may be very hard. You don't always have control, even when you want it.

Even if your childhood has been a succession of problems and issues, you will never forget them, but at the same time if your future life is all about looking back at those problems and issues, consumed with your past, it will be hard to go forward. You must try to break the cycle! You can change the future! You can't change the past.

It is my view that everyone has in fact two lives within their life span. The first life begins at birth, running through childhood into teenage years, reaching its maturity or 'end' before beginning a new life as an adult.

The second life then begins as a new adult, maturing through middle age into old age to reach its finality. Every age evolves from the earlier stage and be special in its own right. It will have its own set of experiences uniquely building your character- the special personality characteristics that make you, *you*.

Think about a cat or dog, or any other animal. At what stage does a kitten become a cat, or a puppy a dog? The crossover from one life to another happens, but it is hard to define exactly when it does. In many ways it is a bit like crossing a bridge – and that is exactly where you are right now.

There also seems to be a parallel between the two lives, which may well explain why we relate so passionately between 'childhood' and 'adulthood', with such a strong emotional tie.

It is therefore very important to value your childhood; to recognize its importance and use your time to learn as much as possible, building not just knowledge, wisdom and respect for other people and the world around you, but also for yourself.

Self-Respect is the single most important and valuable asset you will ever have. It is more important than money, education and all other things.

It is often easier to respect other people's skills, than to respect our own unique abilities and talents and we sometimes don't recognize that we have particular skills, talent and ability.

That is not to say that we need to brag or tell people how fantastic we are! We simply need to recognize and value our own special talents, to see and recognize that we do have them.

Never ever believe that you don't have talent. No one is without talent. It just takes different forms and the time when a unique talent emerges will also be very different.

Absolutely *everyone* has unique skills. There will be things that *you* can do better than others and also things that others can do better than you. Finding your true skills and giving them a value will add enormously to your own *self esteem*.

These skills may be as simple as being able to make good toast or play video games – but they are skills that you have and other people don't.

It is often very hard to work out what skills we have, because we may use them everyday, but not see them as skills. Once you give a *value* to the things you are good at, you will also find that your *self respect* grows too.

Even the things that you are bad at, may well improve as time goes on. There are many people who were at the bottom of their class in early secondary school, who went on to excel in University. A different teacher, a different attitude, a greater motivation, or simply greater maturity can create very different results.

Just because you were weak at adding up when you were in primary school, doesn't mean that you not good at mathematics now or that because you played football when you were twelve years old, that you still love the game! Think about it! Not just your skills, but also your attitudes, beliefs, understanding have all changed and they will continue to change and evolve as time goes on.

There are many adults who were considered 'bad' at school, who have gone on to excel as adults in all sorts of ways. There are also outstanding students who are not outstanding adults. Absolutely nothing is certain.

In some ways it is easy to say, "develop self-respect", but how do you do it? How do you develop confidence, and get others to believe in you too? Some people are very shy and will do anything to avoid being in the limelight, while others will do everything to be in it! We are all very different.

Beating shyness and gaining respect can only come down to your actions – what you say and what you do. It won't happen by itself.

You must work at it at overcoming shyness, and one of the ways is to put yourself in positions where you can't avoid being in the limelight – positions that you may be very uncomfortable in.

Shyness is a way of staying in the shadows, trying not to get noticed. A shy child will try and hide behind their mother's skirts. They are still there but hiding and the main way they do it is by not looking at you. They may even close their eyes.

If you are shy – try and practice looking directly into people's eyes, not away from them.

It may seem hard, but it will become easier. If your typical response when people ask you a question is either "yes" of "no", and no more, then make the effort to say three words instead of one, then aim to say at least six words in reply. The more you talk and respond, the more confidence you will gain.

Be willing to take on a job, even if you are unsure you can do it. The more you push yourself into positions where you have no choice other than to 'do it', the more you will gain a sense of achievement. When you do achieve a success, feel good about it. The confidence will come.

When you look at any famous golfer, tennis player, skier, painter, singer or any other artist or sports person – you can see that they have a real skill in what they are doing.

These people work hard to achieve success through practice, and they also work on *BOTH* their strengths but also their weaknesses. A golfer for example has both a long game and a short game. The long game is where they tee off and hit the ball as far as possible down the fairway to position themselves for the next stage in their game plan. The short game is where they on the putting green, the final steps in getting the ball in the hole.

Golfers must work on both their long game and their short game to succeed – and they will in most cases work harder on their weaknesses than on their strengths. Moral of the story – work on your weaknesses as much as your strengths.

Life has very definite phases. It will certainly have its hardships, and you will not escape this aspect of life. That is reality, and it has been the reality for all people since time began.

Hardships, trouble, arguments, insults, bullying, ridicule will all happen to you at one time or another. You will not escape, but neither should you be intimidated by these events in life, fall over, or allow any of these difficulties to break your spirit. You will certainly be challenged by these events, and the circumstances under which they occurred, and you will also need to learn how to cope with them and how to rise above them. Problems are there to be solved, and everyone faces problems throughout life.

Problems and their solutions are the building blocks of life. They are part of your whole learning experience. Once you solve one problem, the more knowledge you will have to solve the next problem. The more problems you solve, the easier it becomes, and the less intimidated you will be when new problems arise.

No girl or boy, man or woman escapes from solving problems.

Think for a moment of the Queen of England – she's fabulously wealthy and has been famous her whole lifetime from the time she was born. Has she had problems? The answer - of course she has –from personal attacks on her and her family in the media, family divorces, wars, deaths, sickness, constantly having to meet people who she may or may not want to meet.

Every person, from the richest and most famous people on earth, to the most humble and poor, have had to deal with good times and bad, wins and losses, hardship, failure and all the other ups and downs of life on earth.

Think for a moment about anyone you know or have read about - from your immediate family to famous movie stars and ask yourself if you have heard about both hardship and difficulties in their lives as well as their successes.

The reality is that it does not matter who you are, or how famous, rich, poor, tall, short, fat, thin, stressed or beautiful you are, you will face problems in your life. You will also experience success and overcome problems when they occur.

Once upon a time, according to conventional wisdom, all you had to do was to grow up, get married and then live happily ever after! The reality is that this fairytale Prince Charming life never did exist, and even in this fairytale, the princess had to overcome hardship before she lived happily ever after, as did the Prince!

Think about it. Wouldn't life be boring if all that had to do in life is simply exist? Life is always more complex.

There are however certain patterns in life that universally apply to all people.

In a conventional family a baby will be born, then as a child go to pre-school, then primary school, then on to junior high, high school, or college. They may or may not go on to higher education before entering the workforce, doing a job and developing a career.

Emotionally, a baby will first be attached to their parents, then to their siblings (brothers and sisters) and family and as they grow older, they will develop friendships with other people - next door, across the road, at school, wherever they find people whose company they enjoy.

By mid-teens they will have a group of friends and may or may not have formed girlfriend or boyfriend relationships. At some point in the future they may form a permanent relationship, one that results in children, and then the whole process starts again.

These family or relationship structures are pretty much universal, but while the structures are the same, the actual life experiences within these structures will differ markedly from one individual to another.

They will also differ for each family member who grows up in essentially the same circumstances. The first child's experience may well be very different to that of their brothers and sisters. The reasons for this may be many but will have a lot to do with each child's age at the time of certain key family events.

For example, if your parents were divorced when you were fifteen and your sister was three – your recall of the event, and that of your sister will be very different, and the emotional effect will be very different too. Even twins may have a different recall of the same events that happened.

Not all children have brothers and sisters. Many children, and maybe you, are the only child in your family? As an only child, you may or may not have been the centre of attention for your parents. They may or may not have 'spoiled you' by buying you more toys or gifts, even a car because you were the centre of attention. You may have been grateful for this, simply expected this, or been angry about it. You might have felt very lonely or felt that your parents should have given you a sister or brother.

You may also have grown up in a merged family, where you have stepbrothers and or sisters. The relationship you have with your natural parent or parents may be quite different to that with your step-mother or step-father. Love them, hate them or being indifferent to them doesn't change the reality of them being your family. No family, person, or relationship is absolutely perfect.

The victim mentality is not an easy route to take though, and it doesn't give you much in return. All of us are victims in one way or another of events in our childhood. If however your whole life and thoughts are consumed by thinking that you received a really rough deal in your life – your parents got divorced, had to move, couldn't afford to buy special things for you, or even extremes where there was violence, rape, illnesses or other tragedies or events in your life such as a death in the family which you couldn't control – then these events can be become so dominant in your thoughts, that nothing else seems to matter.

"People won't have time for you if you are always angry or complaining"

Professor Stephen Hawking (1942-2018) who suffered Cerebral Palsy and was confined to a wheelchair for most of his life.

It will never be easy, but you must try and overcome the negative thoughts and feelings that surround bad events that happened in your childhood. You cannot control the past, but you can control the future.

This does not mean that you forget, or forgive, or hide away from what happened. It simply means that you focus more on the positive aspects of life – your life – and not so much on the negatives. Not easy, but it is impossible to change what has happened. You have to try to accept that you cannot change the past, as hard as that may be.

The emotions that we had as a child will carry on through your life. You may not talk about certain things or events that happened, but this doesn't mean that you forget them.

You may have been jealous of other kids who had more money, or better looks, or more toys, or lived in a home where there was violence.

Jealousy, anger and envy are part of life, but it can be very destructive if you allow them to consume all your thoughts and actions, dominating your life.

It is easy to let negative emotions overtake you, but would you rather spend your life being angry or thinking nasty thoughts about others, criticizing them, back stabbing and bitching – or simply get on with your own life?

If you radiate happiness, happiness will come to you.

You will always get far greater reward from making positive comments than you will from negative ones. A genuine compliment to someone also makes you feel good. If you are bitching about someone on social media, then recognize that others may also be bitching about you too!

Gossip is a reality, but it doesn't mean you have to have to be part of it or become the carrier pigeon for it through social media or talking about other people.

Everyone has both negative and positive thoughts and it is so easy to become a bully or be bullied. When you set out to be hurtful or superior, does this really bring you any happiness? If you are being bullied by someone, ask yourself what their motivation is and if you decide that they are just being hurtful, drop them as a friend.

If you surround yourself with positive people, that positivity will rub off on you too.

The most beautiful thing in the world is not a dress, or makeup, or moving with the right trendy people or fashions, it is really a smile and the genuine warmth of friendship that you radiate.

People say that the eyes are a mirror to the soul. I think they are right.

Some people's eyes really do shine with their warmth of spirit and you get this almost instant feeling of trust, whereas other people you meet you get an equally immediate feeling that you should not trust them. These are what they call 'instincts' – and it is worth building up a record of your own 'instincts' to see if your instincts were or are the same as the reality.

Some people will leave school at an early age, while others will study for a lifetime. You may well get married, but there again, you may not. You might or might not have children yourself, could get divorced, or maybe stay single. You might have one partner or a hundred. You may get a great job, but equally you might well lose one too! There is simply no single pattern in life.

Whilst there are certainly normal patterns or structures, there is absolutely nothing to dictate that you will or won't, must or must not follow these patterns or structures in your life. Everyone is different, and whether you follow a conventional pattern, or a very different one, will largely be up to you.

CHAPTER THREE

THE INNER AND OUTER SELF

A question of balance

Never underestimate the value of kindness.

It's a question of balance.

Laugh and the whole world laughs with you. Cry and you cry alone.

When you think about yourself, you also think about your family, your friends, your school friends, teachers and other people who have come into your life. Some of these people are very close to you, while others are not, but nonetheless they will all in some way or another have an influence over who you are and the way that you think.

If you have a big decision to take - such as deciding on what course of study to follow, or job to take, you may well discuss these possibilities with your best friends, your parents or others whose advice and experience you value.

No matter how close your friends or parents are to you however, the person you will talk to most with is yourself! Yes, *yourself*. You may lay awake at night, think about the issue or problem to be solved throughout the day and semi-consciously even while you sleep. You will express the positive aspects of each possibility and the negatives. You may well be playing sport, but your inner self may well be somewhere else.

All people have an *outer self* - the part that people see and hear, and an *inner self* that is revealed only to you. Throughout your life, your inner self and outer self will debate forever. You will discuss all sorts of issues, and even things that you will never reveal to any other person.

Sometimes you will find yourself saying one thing, while thinking another, even doing the exact opposite to what you have just said!

You will debate the good and bad points of virtually every action you take in life - and the ultimate course of action you take will be a result of the discussion you have had inside your head.

While everyone does this, very few people recognize the importance of this 'inner self' and 'outer self', as a means of controlling and understanding their own behavior and decision making. Most people don't recognize that they have an inner self and outer self.

The inner self and outer self often display very different personality traits, and it is the balances of these two personalities that will prove very important in your life.

If your outer self is happy, but your inner self is sad, then you will be out of balance. If one half of you is confident, and the other shy or you have great ambition but your outer self hides these away, then you must learn to conquer these imbalances - so that the dominant self stands out. Lack of balance can be self destructive, so it is essential to achieve balance between your outer and inner self.

So how do you use your two selves in a positive way? The first thing is to start thinking like two people and debate the issues before voicing them to other people. Two people always think better than one person, and the more you use the two people within you (your inner and outer selves), the more you will balance your thinking, and better resolve the issues and problems you face in life.

Have you ever wondered why an argument has two sides?

If you look at many of the great achievers in the world – people who may have climbed Mount Everest, or built empires, or become great musicians, actors, sportsmen, Presidents or sailors – what makes them continue to try and achieve new goals, and even more success? Why do very rich people continue to try new ventures, or accumulate even more wealth?

Almost universally, the thing that continues to drive them is the on-going battle between their inner and outer self. This involves a continual battle within themselves to prove that they still have the talent, the ability, the drive, the strength and personality to do what they set out to do. They are not looking for public accolades, for applause, or for people to tell them how great they are. They are looking to prove things to themselves. It is the inner and outer self, playing a game, the game of life - a game that will last a lifetime.

In contrast, people who have lost their will to live because of circumstances around them or have allowed their circumstances to so dominate and pervade their thinking that their inner and outer self both go into a depression state driving themselves downwards and not upwards. Negative thinking, doubts, depression, bad thoughts, seeking to blame others, wallowing in their own lack of success, their bad childhood, old age, bad back, their injury, the struggle of life, the world at war, a rotten job, being poor, being overweight or any other negative thought, all have the same effect. These thoughts do not elevate the spirit or increase your drive or ambition.

The inner and outer self tend to lock out these positive thoughts and drive the feelings into negative territory. They blind the person to all the positive things around them. In fact, the person may try desperately hard not to change any of the things that are causing the negative thinking, in case the changes pull them out of their misery. By creating something or someone to hate or blame, they have the 'monkey' and they don't want to let it go!

There is a classic saying, which has been around for centuries, yet it is as true today as it was centuries ago. "Laugh and the world laughs with you. Cry and you cry alone". While it is easy to get trapped into a cycle of depression you must break the cycle in order to get out of it.

The hardest thing, without doubt is to break out of the cycle. This means changing the focus, the circumstances, facing the problem and doing something about it in a positive way.

Decisions are like closed doors. You may not know what is beyond the door, but in order to find out you must open the door. You will never find out if you don't open the door! Once you have opened the door and gone through it, the door (the problem) is behind you.

The battle between your inner and outer self can help you achieve great things for yourself. Your inner self is your greatest critic but can also applaud you too and be your greatest ally! It can drive you to succeed, and there is no need to feel shy or embarrassed about trying to be successful. If your inner self is saying you can do better, prove that you can. Do better and stop cruising and using other people's success as your guide for measuring your own success. Your inner and outer self will be with you forever, and they can both build your pride and your sense of achievement.

Remember that everyone else has two selves too, a fact that is very important when you're dealing with other people and trying to understand them. Always look people in the eye when you are trying to understand them, because more of their inner self will be revealed. If someone is telling you something that they do not believe in, in other words, only their outer self is talking, not their inner self, then they will avoid eye contact, or make only furtive eye contact with you, in order to pick up on your reaction to what they are saying.

They are trying to pick up on what you are thinking, "your inner self", and will adjust their proposal according to what they pick up.

Traditional psychology says that there are three concepts of self.

First - how you see yourself; second - how other people see you and third - how you perceive other people see you. Strangely all three of these selves are different!

You may see yourself as happy go lucky, yet others see you as serious or your shyness seen as arrogance! Perceptions may be very different to the reality! The eyes however reveal all and are referred to as the windows to your soul.

Your *self* is never a static being. It will change constantly, rising and falling as different moods take hold and situations change. Everyone has moods. Moods are a natural part of life, and we all suffer or enjoy them as they happen. The important thing to remember is that your mood *will* change - a series of peaks and troughs, highs and lows. By recognizing that moods don't last forever and that if you are in a bad mood, then it is simply a matter of time before you come out of it, then you gain a measure of control. That doesn't mean that you wallow in your own bad mood. You can break out of it faster by making yourself busy, and by working out why you're in a bad mood, using your inner and outer self to debate the issue. What was the trigger to your bad mood, or what was the trigger to your good mood?

By using your inner and outer selves and talking in your head openly about your feelings will help. Sometimes people will keep their feelings so closed off to the world that the bad feelings simply grow with the problems becoming so much bigger than they are in reality! The more understanding you have of your moods and the way they form and also change, the more likely you will be able to control the way they swing!

Moods are natural, good and can even be fun. Everyone should get angry at one time or another! In fact, it can be quite exciting, particularly if people don't expect it. No one should be totally predictable!

The question of balance - good moods balanced by bad, also flows to all other parts of life. This is what the Chinese call Yin and Yang.

The principles of Yin and Yang apply to all aspects of life, which says that everything is held in balance within the universe, with everything having an opposite or balancing force. For oceans there is land, for good there is evil, life/death, happiness/sadness, rich/poor, night/day and so on. When we see that it is raining, we know that it is only a matter of time before the sunshine returns. Rather than seeing only the rain, the trick is to look for the sun- to see the good not the bad; the happiness, not the sadness.

When you feel a bad mood coming on, think of this as like a valley. Beside a valley there are always hills or mountains, meaning that a bad mood (Valley) will also be followed by a good mood (Hills). It is simply a matter of time. If you can extend the hills, you will jump the valleys.

Using the principles of Yin and Yang, you can gain a far greater understanding of the world, about what stimulates you, and what doesn't; what's good and bad, worthwhile and not worthwhile; and increasingly as your experience grows, you will learn to see the world more clearly in balance!

This also applies to people you come in contact with. If you look for the good in people you will see it. People are people, so they have their own issues and problems too and what you see is only their outer self not their inner self. If you can break through the shell, you will possibly see and understand more about why they are acting the way that they do.

CHAPTER FOUR
DECISIONS...DECISIONS

Later! Now! Forget it! Why should I?

*It's possible to be brilliant and amazing in one area of one's life
and pretty dim-witted and stupid in others!*

Life's full of questions. Most of these are small. Others are large and have great importance, yet you will be required to answer these questions, taking responsibility for the consequences of your answers. You can also ignore questions, forget about them, delay answering, or return a question with another question.

As an adult you will be making thousands of decisions relating to yourself, your work, your study, your money, your actions, and your future. The way you both think out and answer these questions will greatly influence the way you live and the way you spend your life.

As a child, your parents were making most decisions for you - such as where you would live; what you would eat; where you would be going; as well as earning the money to pay for your schooling, food, and entertainment. Now, as an adult, these decisions will largely be made by you. You may well have to earn your own living.

So, how do you make decisions, and make sure that the decisions you make are the right ones?

The first thing to understand about decisions is that you should see them as simply solutions to problems. In most cases there will be no perfect answer, and usually there are lots of possible solutions.

One solution should however be better than another, but you may or may not hit on this one solution.

Problems ALL have solutions, but what often happens is that people fail to really see what the problem is! They almost guess at the problem or ignore it and therefore end up with a solution that doesn't work, or that misses the point.

With important problems it's important to really spend the time to analyze the problem and understand exactly what the problem is, before rushing for a solution. If you spend a little more time thinking about the problem, you will find that you make far better decisions. First explore the problem and look for alternative solutions, not just the most obvious one. Writing down options can also help too, forcing you to explore the problem and possible solutions in a more complete way. One way to do this is to aim to write down 5 possible solutions, so that it forces you to articulate possible solutions. You can then read over these solutions, think about them and decide your course of action.

The other major mistake that people make is to roll a whole lot of problems into one. In so doing they create a monumental problem that seems impossible to solve. The trick is to try and break big problems into little problems, and then set about solving them one by one. This makes it easy! It's a bit like jumping over little puddles of water, rather than trying to jump a river; or trying to do an exam by answering all questions at once, instead of one question at a time!

Do you relate to this? – *I have an exam to do, my car's just broken down, and I need to pick up a book from the library, but it's closed! By separating the problems, it is far easier to reach solutions.*

Have you ever tried to read a book, by reading every chapter at once? It simply can't be done, yet many people attempt to do this in their lives!

At school it is easy to avoid making decisions, simply by cruising along, doing whatever you really have to, but not getting too involved in any activity.

Taking a backseat in life is also easy and at times everyone does it, but you shouldn't just drift along in life. Pretty much what you put into life is what you will get out.

Again, by using your inner and outer self to debate the issue, you are helping your own understanding of what really motivates you and what doesn't.

If you think about the things you like - for example if you like football, clothes, cooking, skateboarding, or playing computer games - ask yourself what makes it so interesting to you? Why is it that one person can be totally bored watching football while another can watch football for hours on end, while another person who hates watching football, can't wait to get out on the field to play?

The reality is that it doesn't matter what the subject is, it's **the degree of involvement** that really makes the difference!

If you are really interested in something - enthusiastic and involved, then you will get a lot in return.

In contrast, if you are not interested in *something*, whatever that is, and you don't even try to be interested, then you will receive in return virtually nothing. The task will seem harder, the time will pass slower, and you will learn nothing and gain nothing, other than create your own anger and frustrations.

Life should be a passion, and if you are passionate about what you do, value how you spend your time, and approach life full on, then you will get a lot more out of life, and much more than you ever put in.

By giving a little bit more than asked, you will both feel better yourself and your attitude will rub off on others.

Think for a moment about the most exciting thing you did this year. What was the 'central reason' for your excitement? What was the 'crystal', the essential part of what you did that held your enthusiasm, and can you do it again?

One of the most common complaints these days is that people are bored!

Boredom should never be undervalued! That may seem like a strange thing to say, but boredom gives you time to think.

So many people can't cope with boredom and will do almost anything to try and avoid it. If you've been at school where every waking moment of your time has been spent either studying or playing sport, you may well have never spent an hour or a day without people around you! Many schools do this, forcing students to spend every hour in a productive way learning, playing or doing things with others. After the final exams and school is finished forever, these students can often be extremely lost. They have always been organized – seven days a week for sports and other activities, but now must organize themselves - something they have never done before. They have never had to face boredom, and the lack of a strict timetable is very hard on them. It takes many of these former students a long time to recover from this and understand that boredom is a part of life.

If this has happened to you where you have been organized by others for all your life, then that means that the 'problem' has been identified by you. Having identified the problem, you now can find a solution. Without knowing the problem, it would be very easy to jump to very wrong solutions.

While some people absolutely hate being bored and say that they will do anything to avoid it, knowing that boredom makes them depressed or unhappy, they still do nothing to change their situation or the events that are leading to their boredom. Doing nothing means that nothing changes. Non-decisions may defer solving the problem, but it doesn't automatically solve it.

Reality says that you *will* have to cope with being alone at some point, but there is nothing to fear. You're not being abandoned; it's simply time by yourself.

To spend time alone is in one sense a challenge, but it is also a time to get to know yourself, to discover the power within you and the ability you have to rise above the obvious - the boredom you are facing.

Over a period of two years in my twenties I traveled around the world - to Asia, Africa, Europe, North and South America –a great experience, and one that I will never forget.

You see a lot of things, meet people and visit places that become lifetime memories. There are also many times when you wait! You wait in airports, for buses, for trains, for visas and money and a hundred other things! Waiting is boring, but no matter how much you swear, scream, complain, you still wait, so you might as well get used to the idea. You must learn the art of patience, to be able to last the distance, to simply fill the space!

I traveled across the Atacama Desert in South America on the back of an empty semi trailer truck - just myself and two goats with their legs tied together so that they couldn't fall off the truck, surrounded by an ocean of desert sand on both sides of the road.

Nothing to see but the sand! For the first hour or so I kept wondering what the hell I was doing, but gradually I started to see that the desert was stripped of colour. There was just the road, white of the sand and the blue sky with no clouds. By stripping the landscape of its colours- the green of grass and trees, the colours of flowers, people, buildings, it was possible to see the *form* of the land, the *shape* and the textures and shadows created by light. Like a black and white photo compared to color, I was able to see things that I had never seen before. Even today I still think deserts are the most powerful and memorable of all landscapes, and I now look for shapes and textures not just color in the world.

Boredom definitely has great value but its value depends on your ability to see it!

You will not escape boredom, but neither should you try!

So, how do you develop a passion?
How do you decide on what you are really good at doing?
How do you get motivation?

Almost from the time you were born, people want to "classify" you. They may see you hit a ball and say you have natural talent and are bound to do well in sport. They can also declare that you are lazy, dumb, smart, brainy, lousy at math, or a thousand other things, some complimentary, others insulting, and others in-between. These classifications are gross simplifications, because all of us have multiple skills and talents - which evolve, change, and are replaced with new strengths and weaknesses too! Never ever believe that you are dumb, or that there's nothing you're good at! Remember that the smartest people aren't always rich, and the richest people aren't always smart.

Your success might well be recognized by other people, or possibly not! It doesn't necessarily follow that you will get a standing ovation for your achievements.

Ultimately, your successes and failures will be judged by yourself! You are by far the most important judge to consider. You will be the most critical judge, and possibly the most constant critic of your own endeavors. That doesn't mean you have to be hard on yourself. Success is only a measure.

Success may come early or take time. You could well fail once or many times in all sorts of areas. It's your ability to get up and try again that's important.

Throughout your life you will have many successes and failures, and just like an ocean wave breaking on the beach, the successes and failures will come both as small waves and big ones too.

We all develop our intellect in stages, just as our body develops the same way. Everyone, including you, are good at something, and in fact in lots of things.

Right now, ask yourself what you are good at now, and think back three years ago. Were you good at these same things, or something entirely different? The reality is that we all do change, and our interests and skills never remain static.

In our society, people tend to judge success in terms of money and wealth, yet this is just one way. There are many wealthy people who are very unhappy, and many poor people who are happy every day of their life. There is no one single criteria for judging success. You are ultimately your own judge of success.

Motivation, tenacity, belief in yourself, contentment, happiness - they all play a part in your development - not just brainpower. Graduating from university has just as much to do with your ability to keep going to university during your years of study as it does to do with your intelligence. Not going to university has also nothing to do with intelligence!

It's certainly necessary to analyze where your best skills lie - even to the extent of writing them down. At the same time, write down what you think your weaknesses are. The list doesn't have to be particularly long or involved - but from this list you may be able to identify skills and talents you have and skills you can improve.

If you're good at organizing, get involved in activities where you can use this skill. If you are shy, put yourself in a situation where you can't be shy. Try different things. Get involved in activities where you are interested, but also get involved in activities where you are only mildly interested.

By working on *both* your strengths as well as your weaknesses, you will better discover the boundaries to your own skills and learn more as a result. The more involved you are in life, the more you will get from it.

The worse thing you can do is *not* make decisions on the basis that you are afraid of making a mistake. You will make mistakes! You won't avoid making them, and you may well have to pay for the mistakes you make in one way or another.

We all make mistakes, and will often have to pay with our money, time, or apologies, but we also learn through these mistakes. Think about the 'reason' you made the mistake, and when you fix the mistake, ask yourself if you could have found an even better solution to the problem, then the one that you made.

While everyone enjoys seeing people win in sport or other activities, they also like to see how they react when they don't win. Are they a gracious loser, or do they get angry? By far and away the best sportspeople are those who are prepared to acknowledge someone else's success, not just their own.

Life may not be a perfect mirror to a sports field, but the same basic principles apply.

CHAPTER FIVE

STUDY HARD. SURE, WHY NOT!

One of the hardest decisions you make when you leave school is what you want to do. Do you want to study more, if so where, what and how – and even though you may have set your mind on what this is, it may well be that you may or may not get to do that.

This is one of the hardest decisions that you will have to make, and you may have well gone through this whole process already.

If you were not accepted for the course or college that you wanted to go to and had to take up a second or third choice in what you wanted to do. What do or did you do then?

Think of this as a detour. How often have you had to take a detour in life to get to where you wanted to go? Reality is we all make detours at different times in our life, and sometimes these detours end up being more interesting and enjoyable then the original planned trip.

Often the lead up to the decision is harder than making it, but once you have decided, then you will be probably committed to this decision for quite some time.

If you take on a study course, you will be committed to that study course and those subjects for at least the first year. Heaps of students drop out in the first year of college or University. Why?

Gaining a degree or other qualification is not only about being brainy enough to do the course in the first place. It's really about tenacity, being able to stick at it until the very end and achieve what you set out to do.

There are lots of distractions to keep you away from study – friends, parties, jobs, earning money, and the list goes on.

Most students have part time jobs and get money for working. In turn they don't usually get paid to study, and every course of study costs a lot of money plus you need money to live on as well. Apprenticeship trade skill qualifications also mean earning a little while you learn your trade skills and gain a qualification.

Earning money is great, and we all need to do this, but it is also very tempting to just give up on study and go for the job that gives you money now, rather than keep hoping that you will get more money or better, more enjoyable work once you have graduated. These are really hard decisions that you must make – and you will no doubt see a lot of friends go through this, if not yourself.

The chances are that you may also change your mind about what you are studying in the first year. It may not be what you thought it would be, the lectures and/or lecturers are boring, and you "now know what you really want to do". This is all part of the transition from childhood to adulthood.

Think back to school, and you will recall lots of your fellow students going through the same process of deciding about staying at school or leaving to take a job or trying to change courses mid- way through the year. Think about what they decided and what they are doing now. Did they make a good decision of bad?

If I were to give you advice on how to get a degree or other qualification, I would say to make sure you go to every lecture and tutorial and not miss any with an excuse. Yes, this can be boring, but once you start missing classes, you risk making this a habit that will grow, and in turn weaken your resolve to get the qualification.

I would also say to pick subjects that will widen your options, and not limit them, particularly in the first year. While studying may be entertaining and enlightening for some people, most people want to gain some real value from what they are studying, so that they can use in their life. Education is information.

Bear in mind also that there is a very strong lobby group pushing the idea that education is the most important thing in life.

Education is just as much a product as a McDonald's hamburger, and the education business is a big business selling its virtues in the same way as other businesses do. Education comes with a price, and there are high price items and bargain ones as well. What price do you put on getting a "good education"? Is your degree, diploma or certificate valued and if so by who? Also, if you didn't have the qualification, would you be able to do the job you want later or obtain the license to practice the trade or use the skill?

For every decision, there is a consequence or a result. One way of thinking about these sorts of decision points, is to set down two plans of action – a Plan A (stay with the course you are doing) and a Plan B (drop the subject, course and then commit yourself to xyz actions).

Write down the anticipated results (pro's and con's) of each of these plans, and then try and be objective about the decision you take based on what you have set down. Don't try and sell yourself on the answer you want, try to be objective.

Also ask yourself if there is some mid point decision that could limit the risks in any decision you make, for example using some of the credits from your existing course to take to another course, or taking the course part time rather than dropping out completely? You must be realistic and stay strong!

When you are doing your course, look around you and you will probably see older age students doing what you are doing. It is always much easier to get your study years over and done with while you are young rather than come back to it in years to come.

Whatever your decision, try and at least have a plan, rather than no plan. To simply drop out with no plan, to have time out to think more, in most cases is equivalent to no plan at all. Your decision process may well just go around in circles with no outcome resulting.

Talking with friends, parents or lecturers about your plan, lack of plans, questions you are asking yourself is all very therapeutic. It helps enormously, because as you explain your feelings, thoughts and proposed actions with others, they may well raise issues that you hadn't thought about or introduce new thoughts to you.

Often it is hard to talk about these things, as you may think that others will not be interested in your problems, "they don't know what you are going through" or may be critical or judgmental.

The reality is that even if they do not add anything to your thinking, the fact that you have talked about your thoughts will benefit you most. The reason for this is simple. In talking you have *verbally* been forced to put your story across in clear language and in so doing you have had to listen to yourself as well as organize your thoughts into a coherent flow of thinking! So, what will you do?

The worst thing about studying is that it tends to take up all your time. You know that you are studying, while everyone else is out having a good time! Poor you!

Yes, this is reality, but for each small step you take forward, you are moving closer to the end of your study. It takes time, and there's not much you can do about that.

You can however put some balance in your life, by organizing your timetable and week around the lectures you have and plan a timeout period as well. This timeout may be doing nothing at all, playing a sport or doing something entirely different to your normal course of study.

There are lots of activities at most colleges, and in most communities.

Joining a club or getting involved in charity work or sport will mean that you are stepping out of your normal study routine, and through this you will normally meet a different group of people and potentially new friends. It will also help your studies by making you feel fresher for the long hours that you spend on your own studies.

It is normal to have a group of friends that you associate with, but it may also be stimulating to have different groups of friends so that you learn more and find out more about the world around you. Often this occurs when you meet a new boyfriend or girlfriend, where they have a different circle of friends and interests to your own. If you remain open to new thoughts and ideas, you too gain the benefit of this.

CHAPTER SIX
A FAMILY AFFAIR

As much as you are an individual, you are also part of a family.

It is impossible to be born without having a mother and father – be it that your parents conceived you in or through a relationship or within a marriage or outside of one.

Even if your mother was a surrogate mother, a single mother or your father donated his sperm for artificial insemination, you still have a family.

In whatever way that you were born, all be it that you have a natural mother and father, or adoptive parents, a step-mum, step-dad, an adopted family, even a family that you are estranged to or unknown to you – this is your family.

Your family also consists of not just the immediate family you have – brothers, sisters, step-brothers and step-sisters, but also aunts, uncles, grandparents, cousins and the extensions of this – be they blood relatives or relatives by virtue of marriage (the in-laws).

While some families are large, others are small. You may be a single child, or one of many children, have lots of relatives or very few. Every family is different in exactly the same way as you too are different to all other people.

So how do you fit into this? How do you relate to your family? How does your family relate to you? Do you get on well with your family, or are you feeling isolated or rejected, or do you take your whole family for granted.

In the last few years, the divorce rate has dramatically increased to the point where close to 50% of all marriages end in divorce. The reasons for this are many and varied – usually based on frustrations associated within the marriage.

These frustrations may involve lack of romance, money, shared interests, time, success, love, friendship, fun, vitality, boredom, differing ambitions or motivational drives. There may also be factors such as aggression, anger, violence, drugs and alcohol, and of course sexual differences.

There are also divorces caused by affairs or the allure of actually or potentially finding one or some desired qualities in greater intensity with another partner. Every divorce is different, although each divorce may have similar features to others.

When people think of divorce, they usually see it as the breakup of just two people – the husband and wife – yet reality says that it will be the breakup of two separating groups of people – who often but not always take sides in a divorce. When people get divorced, they usually don't see that the divorce will mean that a new group of people will come into their lives – as the husband and wife go their separate ways, and then neither, either or both re-mate with new partners and their associated relatives and friends.

Until the later part of the twentieth century, it was necessary to prove that there was a definite reason for the divorce – such as adultery. No-fault divorces, as defined by the law in most countries changed that.

A divorce can simply be granted due to "irreconcilable differences" and the divorce is granted with custody of any children in most cases, but not always given to the woman, with defined access rights given to the man.

Laws will however vary from country to country and often state by state.

Family Law courts were set up purely to administer and judge the merits, rights and wrongs of each divorce, making decisions in relation to the share and split up of family assets and on-going maintenance payments to pay for the care of children.

All family courts proclaim that their primary concern is the welfare of children – yet children usually are given no voice to say what they want or think. Children will not have control over the situation, and while their wishes may be taken into account, other people will be the decision makers.

Divorce however does affect them, and if your parents have been through a divorce, or you are now part of a new family, then you will know the effects that it has had on you personally. You have also no doubt seen the effect that it has had on your friends too when their parents divorced.

We all desire stability in our lives, and particularly in our family life as it gives us a feeling of security, yet, while this stability may be desired, it is also something that you may not have found.

What divorcing parents usually think about is their own immediate situation, not necessarily through selfishness, simply because their own immediate needs have the highest priority. They are under a great deal of strain and anxiety and emotions are running high.

There will be a parent who initiates the divorce and one who must accept the decision – be it that they do or don't want to. There may well be times of anger, frustration, even irrational behavior as the parents separate their lives, and children including older teenagers may also show the same signs of anger, distress and anxiety.

In the process of divorce, other people become involved – lawyers, friends and relatives. In one way, a divorce can seem like a boxing match, as the protagonists take centre stage and the lawyers, friends and others egg them on – a blood sport to some, fascination or sadness to others.

Often the difference between love and hate is very small.

What divorcing parents don't see is that while they are getting out of one relationship, the likelihood is that they will be entering a new one – where step fathers, step brothers and step-sisters and a new set of relatives and friends will impact on them and on their children.

You may well have knowledge of this – and be part of a merged family.

Merged families involving children from two separate 'prior families' are common and even new children involving your mother and step-father or father and step-mother are now a normal part of life in most societies.

Some of these merged families are extremely happy arrangements, while others are not.

So, how do you cope?

Do you show your anger, or withdraw? Do you talk about the situation, or ignore it as best you can? Do you have feelings of guilt? Who do you turn to? How do you feel about your new brothers and/or sisters? How do you feel about your new stepdad or stepmother, or the boyfriend or girlfriend of your parents?

It is very easy and often the case that you will feel a sense of loss and sadness as your stable world feels like it is collapsing around you. This is a natural feeling.

Divorce and the impact it had on you can be a very stressful time in your life. You are human, and humans come with emotions.

You should however understand that other people have experienced many of the same feelings that you are experiencing now.

While there is no easy way to overcome this sadness or sense of loss or change in your life, the most important thing to do is to talk about your feelings with people who can comfort you.

As we discussed earlier in this book, talking can be very therapeutic, as it is a form of release. Some people find it easy to talk about their feelings, while others will never talk about them – but talking can release some of the pressure that you are going through.

Time and staying busy can also help as it focuses your mind on other activities and interests, so that your whole mind is not consumed with the emotional highs and lows of the divorce that is playing out around you.

One of the great temptations is to feel that you must take sides in the divorce – to see one side as being good and the other bad.

No matter whether you like, dislike, or even actually hate or detest one parent or the other, you will know them for the rest of your life, just as your parents will also know each other in the same way for the rest of their lives too.

While you are probably not in a position where you can directly influence your parent's decisions, you can help by your patience and understanding and not be too judgmental. Remember that your parents too are undergoing probably an even more stressful time than you are.

Families are families – and in the next few years as you develop relationships yourself, you may well start to become a part of your partner's family.

Again, the dynamics of your partner's family will also impact on you.

Your partner's family may be very similar to your own or have very different values to your own. Like it or not when you become romantically involved, and possibly married to another person, this also means that you will also become a part of their family as well.

While we all develop friendships and relationships with other people, ultimately the most important relationship of all is the one we have with our family.

As a teenager you may well have problems that occur – all be it with your career, education, romance, health, money, cars, credit cards, phone bills or other problems.

We all have problems of one sort or another. Problems can also sometimes be embarrassing. If you have managed to crash a car, or run up a credit card debt, become pregnant, drunk or been arrested – there can be a degree of shame or embarrassment that comes with these problems.

While you may feel that "you can't tell your parents", parents and sometimes grandparents will often be the first people that you should tell. Love of a child is the strongest bond of all, and most parents will forgive you, and help you through the crisis. They have more experience in life than you and this may well be the help you need.

Families can be very forgiving, but never take them for granted. Love is a very powerful emotion.

CHAPTER SEVEN

THE HOUSEMATE FROM HELL!

"Solutions never come from an angry mind"
The Dalai Lama

So, you want to move out from home and live with a friend, friends, your girlfriend, boyfriend or new people who you don't know.

At some point you will do this, and it is all part of gaining your independence and leaving the nest. This doesn't mean that you abandon your family. It simply means that you are now an adult and making your own decisions.

Every week, there are ads on-line for houses, units and townhouses to rent, and there are also share accommodation ads looking for housemates.

How then do you choose a place to live, and a housemate or housemates to share with?

Before you move out of home, work out the costs of moving. There may be a rental bond to pay, references to provide (your good character/ability to pay rent), and furniture to buy and the cost of moving to the new place, as well as food and other living costs.

Rent may be paid weekly, fortnightly or monthly. If they ask for a monthly rent, they will usually calculate this by saying the weekly rent is $x, and then multiply it by 52 weeks in the year, and then divide this by 12 to work out the monthly rent. So, as an example this would mean a weekly rent of $100 x 52 divided by 12 = $433.34 per month, not the $400 you thought, thinking a month as being 4 weeks.

Also make sure you know who you are paying the rent to – usually the Agent or the owner of the place. Sometimes (and hopefully never) a flat mate could just pocket the rent you are paying and not pass it on to the agent. Beware.

There are also few legal things you should know.

Houses, units and townhouses are mostly rented out by investors on a lease organized by or through a Real Estate or rental Agent. They will be leased for 6 months, 12 months or longer lease period to tenants that the Agency has appraised (checked up on), based on an agreed rental and payment of bond or key money. The tenant will also have to keep the property in good order too.

Make sure that you know how long the lease is for, as it can be a nasty surprise if the lease finishes or is terminated earlier than you wanted. Also know who is nominated on the lease. If your name is on the lease, that means that you are also responsible for it too –either you alone or jointly with the other persons nominated on the lease.

An agency will also do an appraisal of potential tenants. This appraisal will be based on references given by you (or the group of people to be on the lease – such as you and your friend), as well as credentials to show that you can pay the rent and bond, as well as references that you provide to show that you have previously been a good tenant and that you pay your bills and keep the property in good order.

If you are renting for the first time, it may be that your parents may be asked to be a guarantor for the rent. Being a guarantor means that if a person has not paid the rent, then the guarantor must pay the rent, as they are the guarantor.

In signing a lease, you will be bound by the conditions that are set down on it – eg no pets, payment of key money or a month's rent in advance. This is a legal document. There will be heaps of small print, all designed to tie you up legally if there is a problem. This is all standard practice and protects the landlord from people who run away from paying rent, or damage property when they rent it. It is also designed to protect you as well.

When you have signed a 12 months lease, then you are guaranteeing that you will pay the rent for 12 months, unless there is an out clause, or notice of termination agreement – eg that either party may terminate the lease on 1 month's notice (check the lease document).

If the lease is in your name alone, then you are responsible for the whole lease and rental payments. If it is in joint names, then it is the responsibility of you both, but you will both be responsible for the total rent and condition of the property – both jointly and severally. This means that if your friend skipped town without paying the rent, the onus would be 100% on you to pay all the rent.

A guarantor is also held responsible for paying the rent, if you were both the cease paying the rent for whatever reason. Being a guarantor is not just doing a favor for someone, it comes with the risk of having to pay out in full if there is a default in payment.

There are advantages and disadvantages to be the sole name on the lease. If you are the only person on the lease then you have total control over the property and you can choose who you will share with (sub-lease to). You will also have the right to say who comes in and who is asked to leave.

If it is in joint names (two or more) then you will both or all be listed on the lease and all the parties will be jointly and severally responsible for paying the rent on time. If you fall out with any of these people, or one or more flatmates wanted to move out for whatever reason, then the lease will have to be redrawn with new names – and this with the Agent's agreement. Don't get caught out with your name on a lease when you no longer live there. It still means that you are liable for the rent!

You will also be responsible for the cost of any repairs to the property caused by you or your housemates and their friends.

In choosing a property, there are a number of considerations, the main one being the rent and its affordability, and the condition of the property – its location, size, amenities, age, security, extras etc.

There are always other properties around, so don't think that the place you saw is the ONLY one, and you must have it! There's always another place.

So, how much can you realistically afford? If you work like a slave just to pay the rent, then you will save nothing, and have no money to spend on other things. Not much fun, so try to get your rent as low as you can, and make sure you can pay it on time.

When you are working out what you will be paying each week, also think about transport to where you work or study – both the time and cost and such things as security, noise level, parking, neighbors, closeness to shops, transport, college or work.

In most cases the rent will be established on the basis of the number of bedrooms – with apartments with one bedroom usually being more expensive on a 'per room' basis than apartments with two or three bedrooms.

The more people renting or leasing a property, the cheaper the per-bedroom cost. In other words, sharing a house with 5 people on a rental basis will usually be cheaper per person in rental cost than renting by yourself – depending on the style, location and quality of the rented property.

Sharing with other people however is very different to living at home with your parents. You will have to pay rent, also such things as phones, electricity, gas and of course food and other household needs that you share.

You will also have to supply such things as a bed, wardrobes, a desk for yourself and possibly such things as a TV, washing machine, lounge and fridge. Your housemates may or may not have these and regardless of who owns them, they will be shared and used by all the people sharing.

Sharing with others can be great fun, and you can and hopefully will make great friends sharing with others. It can also be hell if the housemates you have chosen or moved in with have very different values to you! Choose carefully and be aware of what you are getting in to. Even friends who you know very well can be terrible housemates with habits that drive you crazy! You will be sharing a lot of time, but also the toilet, bathroom, kitchen, laundry, car space, fridge, friends, cleaning, conversation, possibly clothes and sharing the bills – electricity, phone, gas, and of course the rent, and the bills *all* need to be paid. Are you willing to share? Will all your housemates do the right thing?

A share house can be very social – particularly if it is a large group in the house. Bear in mind also that each person will have friends, and they will also form part of the extended household – some sleeping over as well.

Everyone is different and have different habits. Some people love to cook, other hate to; some leave the kitchen a mess and the bathroom floor soaked with water; others try and avoid every bill or are always borrowing money; some people are night owls and others early risers and the list goes on.

Choosing the right housemates is therefore critical.

In choosing a new housemate, you need to feel confident that they will fit in with the existing set up. While some people prefer to share with the same sex, or just one other person, other people like to share with lots of other people. Some people would also hate to share at all. It really comes down to you, and what you would like to do.

While you won't want a house mate who is identical to yourself in every way, you will be sharing a lot of time together, and therefore it is important to be able to feel at home. Generally, the more you have in common, the more likely you will get along.

If you have similar interests or activities (eg both working, or both studying, or love sport, music or films), and are of a similar age or background, then you will have something in common, and then work from there. Your judge of people is therefore important.

Housemates tend to move on for lots of reasons, so most weeks there are ads asking for housemates for different households. In most cases the first step is a phone conversation asking for basic information about the flat or house, and the people sharing, and what you are looking for in a house share.

If this goes well, then an interview will be arranged at the apartment or house for you to meet the people and for them to ask you about yourself. This is the time for you to ask about the existing people in the house or flat, and the arrangements for paying the rent, for food etc. You will, just by seeing the kitchen, bedroom and bathroom gain a feeling for the house and people living there.

Some of the questions you might ask would cover – the room itself; the rent and how it is paid (eg weekly or fortnightly); the bond; electricity – possibly they put money aside in a kitty; who holds the lease, how long they have on the lease, who is living there – number, length of stay, age, gender, what they all do (unemployed? work? study?); parking arrangements; washing, TV, how they buy food; how they share cooking and cleaning; what they like and don't like in a housemate (eg drinking, smoking, drugs); issues like boyfriends/girlfriends staying over; if they do or don't socialize together; security (keys, locks, insurance), as well as what you can bring to the house (eg a washing machine, TV, skills or talents).

If you like the bedroom, general feel of the place and the people, then say so. If you don't, then make your excuses and go on to find a place that better suits you.

House sharing can be great fun, and a great way to meet a variety of people. Everyone who has shared an apartment or house will have their own stories – some funny, some sad, some bizarre, even romantic stories of housemates sharing more than just the rent!

So, how do you avoid the housemate from hell? Unfortunately, there are a number of housemates from hell, including the druggies, drunks and egotists.

Housemate from hell – type one *is the person who doesn't pay the rent or tries to wriggle out of paying bills. If they don't have the rent, or are always late paying it, it becomes a total pain to live with them, as the onus for paying always rests on the others. The even worse type one housemate is the one who disappears leaving a massive bill behind, with the account held by one of the others in the house. That's why it's important to have a bond paid by everyone in the house.*

Housemate from hell – type two *is the person who leaves the place always in a mess – be it the kitchen, the living areas, bathroom or laundry. If you like living a pig sty, that's fine, if not, beware! Also remember that if the place is damaged, eg wine spilled on carpet or cigarette burns, this will be an expense you may not want.*

Housemate from hell – type three *is the invisible housemate, the one who's never there. She or he stays at their girlfriend or boyfriend's place and contributes nothing to the household in personality or friendship. The opposite can also be painful, if the boyfriend or girlfriend is always living in your house, and not contributing at all to food or other expenses.*

Housemate from hell – type four *is the room dweller penny-pincher who likes to live in isolation, and is sharing purely to keep their expenses low, with their whole focus being to always spend as little as possible! They take, but never give, and they may well have their separate shelf in the fridge for "their own stuff". Watch out for these types.*

Housemate from hell – type five *is the ever present, non-stop ever talking, in your face, pain in the neck type who you can never avoid, who wants to know where you are, what you are doing, when you'll be back - the busy body from hell!*

Housemate from hell – type six *is the party animal that loves to party every night and bring in the crowd to crash out at your place. Parties are great fun, but not every night.*

Housemate from hell – type seven *is the super bitch! Some girls get on well with other girls, and some don't! A house full of girls only can get very bitchy, just a house full of guys can get very 'male'!*

You will be sharing with all of them and living with them. If there is anger or hostility in the house, it affects everyone.

And then there are the angel housemates, who far outnumber the ones from hell – who you may well know for the rest of your life. You will share lots of laughs with them, and they may well know more about your love life and everything else about you than anyone else!

House sharing can well be one of the best times of your life. The main complaints arise when people don't pay their rent on time, or the bills on a shared basis, or don't do their fair share of cooking, cleaning or other chores. Sharing means exactly that, and that means sharing both people's good habits and bad.

CHAPTER EIGHT
STARTING A CAREER

Love your job…love life

Keep your options open.

As a teenager, one of the greatest uncertainties relates to the career that you are likely to follow and the uncertainty of not knowing whether you will or won't get a job. You will. It just takes time!

While there are certainly people who know exactly what they want to do, most people really don't know, and even those who do, may or may not go into their chosen career for one reason or another.

One of the great myths that we grow up with is that once you have chosen your career, that this will be your career for life! That simply isn't the case.

In fact, you are likely to have several careers, or job roles, often miles apart in their work type and style. Your change in career could well be due to technology changes, changes in the marketplace, changes that you initiate in your lifestyle, or due to other people or circumstances that arise for whatever reason.

You may study to be a baker, but move onto real estate, or graduate as an architect and become a horse breeder. Careers can be quite diverse, but jobs are even more so! You may well take on a career that currently doesn't exist.

Millions of jobs in marketing, computers, software application, entertainment, health and welfare simply didn't exist even five years ago. So, if the job doesn't even exist, how do you plan for it? What do you study, or even more importantly, what don't you study?

Often when you look at some of the subjects you have at school, you wonder why you're studying them. How can theories of relativity or probability, or poetry, physics, or ancient history help you in the life you have ahead? Fact is that directly they won't, but they will give you a diversity of experience and knowledge, and let you know that there are areas of study that lie beyond the area of knowledge you have. They will also teach you the ability to solve problems, to remember, to link diverse thoughts together, isolate arguments and establish viewpoints - ie the ability to rationalize and think.

Is a Medical Doctor going to be better at his or her job, if he or she has some knowledge of building, or has worked in a restaurant? Certainly, a Doctor will have patients who come from all walks of life, so having some experience in the restaurant trade or building won't go astray. It may well add more understanding and empathy, thereby making their judgment of a problem and finding a solution more complete.

Experience is all about knowledge, and the more diverse your knowledge, the more likely you are to make better decisions, and be in better control of your own destiny.

When you finish school having completed your final exams, a lot of people choose to take a year off to decide what they want to do – a gap year.

The belief is that in so doing, they will discover at the end of this time exactly what they want to do. With places very hard to obtain in universities and colleges, the chances are that they could well waste a year and could well be less motivated than they would have been if they had decided on a course at an early stage when the opening was there. Making decisions, even if you get it wrong is better than not making one at all.

For some people a gap year can be a good decision too as they grow one year older and hopefully learn about life and what they want to do. Gap year of no gap year is an individual decision.

As you go through your teens, taking casual jobs whenever they become available builds your knowledge of people, processes, business activity and other things. This all adds up to experience and will help you better form judgments on the types of jobs that are available to you. It will also make you more employable, because it develops your own self-confidence.

Imagine if two people turn up for a job interview, both with the same education. How will the future employer choose between them? The judgment will come down to such things as personality, presentation, interest shown, enthusiasm, drive, and the extras shown on your resume, such as previous jobs, involvement in community and sporting activities, and other such things.

If twenty people turn up for the job, your chances of success diminish. It then becomes a matter of standing out and making sure that the potential employer remembers you. It's almost certain that the potential employer won't remember all twenty people who they have interviewed. That may sound somewhat harsh but place yourself in their situation. Would you remember twenty people that you have just met?

This means that you need to work hard to stand out in the crowd! Again, the same basic principles apply - and the more you make an impression the more likely you are to be short listed for the job.

Details matter! If there are spelling mistakes in your resume, or the information is jumbled, these will be demerit points before you start - so take the time to set out a good resume - something that you are proud to show to anyone who needs to see it. Don't be afraid to show other people who could add to what you are saying in the resume and get their advice and input. If someone offers to help, take the person up on the offer. An introduction is always better than no introduction at all!

When you are young you won't have a lot of experience to offer - but that shouldn't mean that your resume should be a blank piece of paper! It simply means that you need to be creative!

So how do you write a resume that is interesting and memorable?

Firstly, there are no guarantees. You may hear back. You may not! Not all employers know exactly what they want, and not all will be organized; be professional in the way they approach employment; or indeed are all that interested in you or anyone else! They may simply be fishing, seeing who's available, or just doing their job! This is not to discourage you, but simply to wake you up to the reality that people all have different motivations, including employers and personnel agencies. If you want the job, you need to show your enthusiasm and talent to the employer, which firstly means getting through the door to get an interview.

Your first job is therefore to get the interview in the first place - so if you have managed to get an interview, then recognize that you have already achieved success. A lot of people didn't get short-listed or even get an interview, so give yourself a pat on the back. If you didn't get that far, then change your approach or take a salesman's approach based on numbers - the more doors you knock on, the greater your chances of success! In other words, if you didn't get a response, then you haven't knocked on enough doors!

So, apart from the obvious - your name, address, contact phone number, and e-mail, you will need to list your education achievements and employment background. These are the most important items - but also try to make them as interesting as possible. Remember you're trying to get the interviewer's attention, hold it and get them to shortlist you for the job! Think about the job you are going for, and ask yourself what you think they are looking for? What do you think would be of interest to them?

If you did well in a subject, then tell them, as well as saying why you liked the subject. Show enthusiasm. Try to get your personality to shine through. Never tell lies however! If you worked somewhere, list the name of the company, and what the company does, as well as what you did when you worked there. While you know the company, the interviewer may not. By saying what the company does, you are building your own creditability as well, because while the reader does not know you, they will probably know the company or companies that you have worked with. Even if they don't, you have built your own creditability by talking about the company you worked for.

Compare the following resumes-

RESUME

Name: John Smith

Date of Birth: 10th March 1983

Address: 301 Port Road, West Highland 2187

Tel: 983-8765

Email: jsmith@joker.com

Education:

Higher School Certicate – subjects being English, Advanced Mathematics, Computer Studies, Biolgy, Chemistry, Language Studies, History

Nationality: American

Employment History:

Worked in a shop part time for past two years

Personal assessment:

I enjoy playing netball, and at school my best subject was English.

I would like to find a postion where I can use my sporting knowledge.

References:

Mr John Sakato Tel 657 4777
Ms Fiona Warren Tel 993 2226

This resume is way too short! The reader will basically pass it over because it simply doesn't say enough. It also has spelling mistakes in it (underlined), which also means that the person seeking the job is either lazy or is really not very interested in finding a job. Don't make these mistakes!

In contrast, read the following-

Same details as above, but without the spelling mistakes, and with details of employment history -

Employment History -

Although I have been studying for the past five years, I have also been working part time work in a retail clothing store.

The store, called "Macho" sells men's and women's fashion clothing. I was employed in a part time sales role with some administration work involved, reporting the day's sales to head office, opening and closing off the cash register and store at the end of each day's trading, marking off staff hours, and ensuring general security was maintained.

I worked during a number of sales promotion periods, including Christmas, and took on the role of organizing the window displays, as well as making recommendations on selection of stock to sell.

Through this job I have gained a good knowledge of the retail trade, and …..(detail other things you learned which might be valuable to the employer ie if you're going for a admin job, then emphasize your admin skills; if a sales job, then emphasize your admin/ computer skills) Remember there is always something you can say!

Personal assessment -

While I don't have a lot of experience, I do enjoy meeting people, and learning as much as possible about the things I do. My passion is netball and I have played at both school and club level winning …

(details). I am very much a team player, and I would love to work with (name of company). I feel confident that I would be able to handle the job, and I am willing to do whatever is necessary to build up my knowledge and job skills.

This resume has essentially the same information as the first, but the reader will have a far better impression of you if they have read the second rather than the first resume. You should try to convey a picture of who you are, without being boastful, or overstating your abilities.

Remember too that one of the most critical factors in deciding upon whether you get the job or not, will be the interviewer's assessment on how you will or won't fit in with the people who currently work for the company.

If you have a portfolio of some of your work, or projects, have it ready to take with you should you be successful in getting an interview. Also think about what questions *you* will be asked at the interview.

Ask about the company, what it does, who you will be working with etc to show that you are interested in the company and the people who work there!

With your references, don't just list the name of the person who will give you a reference, as per the first resume shown here. Say who they are, for example. Again, it *adds* to your creditability.

eg
Mr John Sakato – *Managing Director of Boris Motors, West Highland's leading Toyota dealership.*

I have known Mr Sakato for 6 years, and he has coached me in netball for much of this time. I also spent two weeks work experience with Boris Motors. Mr Sakato has agreed to provide a reference for me and is happy for a potential employer to phone him in relation to my skills and character. Tel 657 4777

Here you have shown your relationship to Mr Sakato and by providing details of Mr Sakata, you have added to his creditability as a reference, as well as enhancing your own.

So good luck! A good resume will boost your confidence, and greatly improve your chances of getting a job. Other techniques you can try to use are a distinctive type face (a business style, not too decorative); a different color paper (to stand out more); and a cover sheet to add extra style and 'bulk out' your resume, so that it looks more impressive. Often a photo of yourself will help too. Most resumes will be sent by email, more so than on paper, but the same rules apply.

Once you have the job, try to build up your skills as fast as possible. The more knowledge you have about the job you are doing, the more confidence you will have, and the more you will be in control.

How long you stay in a job really depends on you. While there will certainly be jobs that you don't enjoy, there will also be ones that you do.

The best job is one that doesn't feel like a job at all, and jobs like this do exist! If after you have been with a company or organization for say three to six months, and you find you are still not enjoying it, then look for another job. There's nothing worse than feeling miserable at work. It is however financially smarter to look for another job, while you have one, rather than making yourself unemployed, and then looking for a job!

CHAPTER NINE
THE DANGER YEARS

How to survive

The age 17 to 25 is the most dangerous time in your entire life. These are the years when you are most at risk - and that risk largely comes from speeding, drugs, alcohol, cars, motorbikes and taking risks involving you, your friends and the people you meet.

You may well be the safest driver in the world, but if you hop into a car where the driver is high on drugs or alcohol, sleepy or speeding, you could well be killed. An innocent party, but dead nonetheless!

The danger is very real.

So, how do you protect yourself?

As a driver, you know all about the road rules and that the main dangers involve speed, alcohol, falling asleep, driving when tired and disobeying the road rules. You can also add to the list, tailgating the car in front (driving too close), driving through a red light, aggressive driving and over confidence.

Everyday that you drive, you are taking a risk, but you can eliminate most of these risks if you want to.

Driving very much relates to attitude as well as skill.

Crashes happen in many cases between one car and another. If you avoid being too near other cars, you most likely won't run into them, or they into you!

That not only means keeping a safe distance from other cars yourself, but more importantly it means *anticipating what the other drivers are going to do before they do it.*

There's absolutely no doubt that other drivers will do things that are crazy, but if you are away from them when they do it, then you will stay safe and your car won't be smashed up.

There are good drivers and bad ones and you will see drivers doing things you can never quite believe.

A great number of accidents happen on corners with a car not going around a corner safely instead heading into a tree or other obstacle.

Driving too fast, being distracted, trying to send a text message and not concentrating on the road can all lead to accidents.

Don't look to enforce the road rules yourself. The worst thing you can do is become angry, because it will make your behavior irrational, and possibly aggressive.

When it comes to moving out into a moving line of traffic, just think to yourself "Is there a risk in doing it?" If there is, then wait the extra minute or so.

If you eliminate the risk, you eliminate it possibility of crashing.

A good way to avoid getting angry is to count out numbers 1 to 20 slowly in line with breathing, trying to slow down your angry reactions. Also try and smile and see the funny side of what has happened.

I remember recently seeing a truck driver at about 7 o'clock in the morning yelling at someone in a car who had cut them off. This guy was extremely angry, but the reality was he probably had a whole day of driving to do – all ahead of him. Can you imagine feeling that anger all day long?

Motor Bikes are even more deadly than cars. The reasons for this are simple. Firstly, you don't have the protection of a lot of metal around you, and a bike, being just two wheels is far more likely to slip around on the road, and if it hits something, it will most likely send you over the handlebars at whatever speed you were traveling.

Bikes also have much more acceleration then cars, and that power can get you into lots of trouble fast. While you may have a license for a 125cc motorbike, the temptation is to ride a bigger bike and go faster. Probably the police won't be checking your license which means there is a great temptation. More power means even more acceleration and speed, and more danger.

When you hit something, it is the *force* that causes the problem. Force is your speed multiplied by your weight.

I remember hearing of a bike rider who was smoking a cigarette and racing at the same time when he hit a tree. His cigarette was imbedded into the tree trunk! That's the meaning of force.

If you must have a motorbike for the freedom and exhilaration, and lots of people do, but you want to stay safe, then absolutely, your safety comes down to *attitude* – yours.

Nothing is there to protect you on a bike. Even if you are totally innocent and not breaking any road rules, or another driver is absolutely in the wrong, you will be the one who will be hurt in an accident. That could mean a broken leg, or getting steel pins put into joints that have been smashed or suffering months in hospital.

It could also leave you as a paraplegic.

On a bike assume that people don't see you and will not give way. You must contend also with the road, and even if there is oil, ice, grooves, a huge hole in the road, or even a bolt lying on the roadway, it will be *you* who will be damaged.

No one is there to look after you, only you and it may well be your attitude the thing that will either protect you or kill you!

There are courses run by very experienced riders, who will teach you the 'art of living' with a bike, and there's lots of enjoyment that you can get from riding, but remember the danger, and act accordingly.

That all seems harsh, but it is hard to avoid the reality that motorbikes and cars kill more young people then they do older people. Some insurance companies won't insure young drivers due to the high risk they pose.

Speed and adrenalin go hand in hand, and they might seem innocent, but they take many victims!

You know pretty well that society says: "don't drink and drive", "don't do drugs", "don't speed", "speeding kills", "there's no such thing as safe speed", and all the other ad lines!

At the same time, you have probably enjoyed driving or been in a car driving fast rather than slowly; possibly enjoyed the effect of alcohol making you feel good; and maybe either seen people who have taken drugs or taken them yourself.

The next few years will be probably the best "party times' that you are ever likely to have. Having left school, you will be meeting a whole lot of new friends and probably going to pubs, rave parties, music gigs, late night movies, as well as maybe buying your own car so that you will be more mobile than ever before. It's an exciting time in your life.

If you're at a party, the main thing you will want to do is 'have a good time', and that's a pretty natural thing to do. You will also come into a lot of peer pressure from your friends and even just acquaintances to drink more and try drugs. They will want to share the experience, get you involved, and into a party mood. This pressure can be intense at times and they will continue to try at different times, not just once to get you to just have another drink or just try taking a tablet that will give you a high.

With alcohol, the danger is not so much from the alcohol itself but from the high that the alcohol gives you, which means you can do things you wouldn't do if you were sober.

Alcohol affects people in different ways. Some people simply get in a very happy mood - laughing, giggling, dancing, talking, getting rid of their shyness, while others can get violent or aggressive - wanting to pick fights, hurt others. The second group is the one to avoid, and if you find yourself in this category, be tough on yourself as to when you drink, what you drink, and how much you drink.

The way to stay sober and not get a huge hangover is firstly not to mix your drinks - don't have a mixture of vodka, beer, red wine, white wine - just stay with one of these. Pace yourself.

If you want the alcohol high, but don't want to get drunk, have a glass of cola or water every second drink instead of the alcohol and towards the end of the night switch over to water only. You can still get the alcohol 'feel-good' high at the beginning of the night, but by the time you leave at the end of the night, you will be back to being reasonably sober. The more water you drink before you go to bed the less hungover you are likely to be in the morning too!

The big danger period is when everyone decides to go home at the end of the party. If you're drunk or just feeling tipsy, you could well just get in any car that's available without knowing if the driver is sober or not. In the car you only need one person to encourage the driver to 'go faster', or 'do a burn-out for the driver to speed or start to do stupid things. If you don't feel good about a car or a driver, then don't get into the car!

I little while ago, I went to the funeral of the son of a friend of mine, killed as a passenger in a car that hit a tree.

It was one of the saddest funerals that I have ever been to – the pall bearers carrying the coffin had heads bandaged and arms in slings, the crowd a mixture of his friends from college, parents and relations all in shock. The pallbearers had survived the crash but been in the car. Their friend died, and they had survived, but they were unlikely to ever forget the tragedy that had occurred. The boy's parents were also in a state of shock. No parent ever wants to see the death of their child.

Before you head to a party, plan ahead so you know how you will get home and ideally who you will come go home with, and drink lots of sodas or water. At most parties there will be a surplus of alcohol, but not enough soft drinks. If there isn't any soda, there will always be water from the tap! Even at pubs and discos, there will always be water in the bathroom.

The thing about drinking is that people drinking want everyone else to drink too! If you drink water, just do it, but don't make a any issue of it, or you won't have just one person hounding you to drink more, but everyone at the party!

At the end of the party, you could also find that your friend who was to take you home, has found a new girlfriend or boyfriend, and that they are going on somewhere else. This happens often, so pre-plan for it. Always have a cell phone and some emergency cash put away somewhere, as your 'no-touch' emergency money, so that if you need to take a taxi, then you have enough money to do so. These are your security blankets- your safety net.

While alcohol can get you into problems, it is to some extent controllable, as you consume it one glass, can or bottle at a time. Drugs however are much more unpredictable and can get you into trouble much faster.

Drugs are by and large easy to take and will give you a faster high. They all effect the brain and will alter the way you see the world when you are high. They are also made up of chemicals.

While smoking occasional marijuana joint may or may not give you 'a high', smoking marijuana constantly *will* take away your drive and ambition and make you lethargic. You probably won't pick this up, but others will. Drifting along doing nothing, thinking about things too much, dropping out of college so that you can think a bit more about what you want to do in life, all these things are things that will happen to you if you start using too much dope. It won't happen to everyone, but certainly this is a definite side effect of repeated use.

The heavier drugs like ecstasy, cocaine, speed, ice and others and the no-go zones like heroin all cost lots of money. There are so many drugs around and taking any pill or substance without knowing what is in it, will put you at risk.

They may also affect you emotionally in ways that you never thought possible. There are many people in psychiatric hospitals because of drugs. There are also pills made using all sorts of chemical compounds and when pill-testing is done, they find all sorts of chemicals in them, from rat poison, bath salts to cement.

While a pill might be safe, it is also possible that it is not and you take a big risk and endanger your own life if you do swallow a pill. Why would you gamble on it being safe to take?

MDMA pills or capsules alter moods and perceptions, increasing your heart rate and energy levels and distorting the reality around you. Many people take these drugs before heading to a music festival and take the drug along with alcohol or other drugs, but you are always taking a risk.

You have no doubt heard that people have died from an overdose at music festivals. What you don't hear so much is about brain injuries and heart attacks brought on through over dosing of even prescription drugs too.

There are young people who having taken a drug, simply jumped off a building thinking they could fly and others who thought they could run across a highway through the traffic. Drugs distort reality.

If you think it is tough to say no to drugs in the first place, imagine how much harder it is to get off them, once your body and your mind are both saying you want it, and your dealer is pushing you to buy more. They don't call them pushers for nothing.

Drug pushers are there for two reasons. One they are out to make money, and the more people who buy from them, the more money they make. Their second motivation is even worse. They don't value your life, because they don't value their own. They are quite happy to hurt you, to get you addicted, and they may well enjoy the *power* that this gives them over you. They themselves may have been hurt in the past, and therefore they feel they have every right to hurt you too.

Who cares if you get hurt, or even die! To them you're the sucker…and when you are really hooked, then you're just "scum", "another bloody junkie".

Would you really like someone to have this sort of power over you?

Heavy drugs also lead you into real problems like lack of money, and the need to get money through illegal means. Not fun and to break the habit, maybe impossible. To see a druggie lying in the gutter, eyes bulging out, matted hair and clothes hanging off them, is perhaps one of the saddest sights you can see in a city.

Ask yourself if you really need to do drugs to have fun? As an adult you have a choice, and it really is your decision. Do you really need to take a risk? If all your friends are taking drugs, does this mean you have to too? If they won't invite you to parties, because you don't do drugs, will you be strong enough to find other friends?

Staying clear of drugs when they are so freely available is not easy, but as an adult you are the one in charge. You can't really blame your parents, or school or someone else if you decide to get involved. It also won't solve any emotional problems you have or make you more attractive.

Ice is also anything but cool. In some ways everyone wants to be a 'superman' to do things that no-one else can. In normal life you see a normal world, but what if under the influence of 'ice' that world was an alien place, that the people you saw were all monsters determined to destroy you, so you struck back to kill them and throw them off the balcony or stabbed them with a knife.

Imagine then the next day you then discover that the monsters you fought so strongly against were your parents, or nurses and doctors in a hospital. How would you feel then?

Ice is bad news. You may take it thinking it will enlighten you, give you pleasure, your friends have taken it without problems and all the other rationales that you might put forward, but aren't you smarter than that?

Don't get sucked in.

Remember too, that if you associate with druggies, the more likely you are to become one too. Choose your friends and company wisely.

You must stay strong, and when you do, give yourself a pat on the back. Stay strong and build your own self-respect.

Being a teenager, means you feel you can do anything you set your mind to do, and you can.

Now should be the most exciting time of your life when you take on the world and discover all that it has to offer. Just be aware of the dangers. You can survive the danger years, but you should be aware that these next few years are the most dangerous years of your life.

CHAPTER TEN
ANOREXIA, BULIMIA AND THE QUESTION OF WEIGHT

As a teenager, you have already been through a lot in life. You have taken lots of exams over the last few years. You have also seen your body change from that of a child into an adult and have also maybe had to experience pimples on your face, maybe dandruff in your hair, and a whole lot of other issues that you have had to deal with.

Many teenagers and young adults suffer from pimples and acne and in most cases this is hormonal. There are lots of pharmacy products that can help, but if it gets bad, see a doctor or cosmetic or skin specialist. Don't just leave it to chance as it can leave to scarring.

These are all problems that you can overcome, so you should feel good about yourself and the achievements that you have made so far. You deserve to be congratulated and feel proud of yourself!

Alas, once you have overcome one problem, there are always new ones to handle!

One of these is your body appearance and weight.

What do you do if you feel that you are too skinny or too fat or want to be taller, shorter or have more shape or other change?

It is normal for people to compare themselves with others, and people throughout history have always played with their appearance by changing their hair styles, creating wigs, wearing platform heels or stilettos to get greater height, wearing corsets to gather in their waist lines and a host of other things to make themselves more attractive, or sometimes less attractive to others.

In Africa and in Asia they sell products to lighten the color of the skin, while in lots of Western countries people spend a fortune trying to get a 'tan' and look darker. Short people want to be tall, and tall people want to be short!

While there are many things that we can do easily to change our appearance – like changing the clothes we wear, or our hair style, the main thing we can do is change our attitude about the way we feel about ourselves.

How we *feel* emotionally about ourselves is far more important than how we *physically* appear.

While it seems the world concentrates on *beauty*, the thing that most attracts us most to another person is *personality*. Personality wins hands down, as does having the right *attitude*.

Don't obsess about your looks. If you are spending hours in the bathroom preparing to go out, you really have a problem. Confidence comes from action – going out, not standing in front of a mirror and analyzing every freckle on your face, or combing your hair endlessly, and worrying about what people will or won't say about you.

People are much more attracted to someone who has a smile, than someone who thinks that a beautiful dress and makeup will outshine a scowl on their face.

There may be two people with identical weights – one looks very stylish, while the other looks frumpy. The difference is in their attitude, how they feel about themselves, and how they dress and portray their personality to the world.

That doesn't mean that we should try and look ugly, but there are people who want to do this too!

Think about some of the music stars who have naturally good looks, but go all out to make themselves look tough, rugged or aggressive. Beauty is all about perception.

You will no doubt have seen tall people who are hunched over when they walk. What they have tried to do is to look shorter, but instead of being shorter, they have ended up with hunched shoulders!

If you are tall, be proud of it. There is no need to be apologetic. Lots of people are desperate to be tall, just like you!

Similarly, if you are short so what? There are lots of people who are human dynamos, who are short in actual height, but tall in all that they do. Just be proud of who you are.

While one person is desperate not to be noticed, another is desperate to be seen.

You have also probably seen a very large person dressing in a size too small for them – stretching the fabric as far as it will go. While they themselves are trying to convince the world that they are a smaller size, the world simply sees a large person in clothing too small for them. Which is better – dressing in a size too small, or dressing in the right size, and doing it with style?

In society there is a total preoccupation about weight, and the problems associated with it.

While physically we all need food to eat, food also provides a means of comfort to us.

In a physical hunger sense, we don't need desserts, but what the dessert does is give us a sweet end to the meal. Do you remember threatening that you wouldn't get your dessert unless you ate your main meal?

There are all sorts of foods that can be classed as *comfort foods* to us. Most are sweet like chocolate, confectionery and ice cream, and during the day we tend to seek out these types of foods.

Junk food high in fats and salt also fall into this category.

The trouble is that these same foods are also the ones that are nutritionally the least good for us.

For a lot of the time, we don't eat because we are hungry!

We just eat because we are bored; It's time to eat; others are eating or food smells or looks good at the time.

Eating food, even bad food, is very much a habit, and if you know that you are eating the wrong things, then it is up to you to change. No one is just going to do this for you.

By habit it may be easier to grab a hamburger and fries to eat, rather than a salad or fruit, but once you get into the habit of eating fruit and natural foods, the chips and burger may seem less attractive.

Food stalls are there to sell food, and therefore set out to get you to buy. Why do you think confectionery is right beside the cash register; that fast food is so convenient; and that they have back lit signs showing highly appetizing hamburgers above the counter?

In times of recession when people are worried, sales of chocolate and confectionery rise, as do alcohol and cigarettes. The reason is very simple. People are looking for comfort, for simple things that will provide comfort to them in a time when they are stressed. It is a psychological need, and not a physical need.

While all of this is rational and understandable, there is a lot of pressure on us to fit in with what we perceive are society's physical appearance expectations of us.

People can also be particularly rude and insulting in relation to how others look. They brag about themselves, compare themselves with others, insult and generally bitch about anything and everything that is to do with people. It is easy to be affected by this.

All of us will have seen this happen at different times at school, and it is no different in a work environment.

For girls, particularly in their teenage years, who have periods each month playing with their emotions and hormonal changes taking place, the need to look right, feel good and fit in with the crowd can be very stressful.

Dieting and weight control can become an obsession.

While teenage girls are not the only ones to suffer these obsessions, they are the ones who suffer the most, and in the USA, Britain and a number of other countries 'eating disorders' have reached epidemic proportions.

'Eating disorders', like Anorexia nervosa, and Bulimia can last from one to fifteen years, and over 86% of people who suffer from these eating disorders started having the problem in their teens.

This is a really serious problem.

So, what's the difference?

People who suffer Anorexia Nervosa basically starve themselves, so that even though they will feel hungry, they deny this and refuse to eat, believing that if they eat, they will become fat! They will also often do exercise on a compulsive level, again to keep their weight down. Anorexia sufferers have a total phobia about becoming fat, and in extreme cases will even starve themselves to death, or become so weak that they must be force fed.

Bulimia sufferers will eat, and may appear to have normal weight, but will have alternate routines of fasting and binge eating, using laxatives compulsively and inducing vomiting to get rid of the food within them. Bulimia sufferers will also go to great lengths to hide the fact that they are doing this.

There are also people who both suffer Anorexia and Bulimia, starving themselves, as well as taking laxatives and self inducing vomiting to get rid of anything that they have eaten or been forced to eat.

Compulsive overeaters or binge eaters, when they are depressed will turn to food as a comfort, and binge on whatever food is available at the time. The overeater may have normal meals, or larger ones, and then go on to have a late-night binge, or 'pig out' on chocolate or any of their favorite foods. They will as a result put on weight and create a cycle of 'depression' because of their weight, and 'bingeing' to get over their depression!

Remember when we talked about the *inner* and *outer* self?

What is happening here is that the outer self is saying to the world at large, 'look at me, I don't have a problem', while your inner self is tormenting the hell out of you, creating a secret world of denials, self deception and lies, which become a cycle which is extremely hard to break out of.

These problems are all psychological. That is not to say that they are not real. In fact, they are very real, and need to be treated very seriously, as these conditions will directly affect your health and well being.

Starving yourself is a bit like running a car with no oil. You will gradually stuff up your whole engine!

The body depends on regular food in order to function. Starving yourself will mean that your muscles deteriorate, you will become easily tired making you extremely moody, and blood pressure can drop to the point where you can faint or pass out. Long term damage can occur if you don't do something about the Anorexia and see a doctor or Dietician about your problem.

It is all too easy to deny that you have a problem and you are not alone! In the United States alone there are around 7 million women and about a million men who have some sort of eating disorder.

If you are using laxatives or constantly trying to vomit your food up to stop weight gain, then again think about what you are doing. It is not normal, and you need to get professional help.

Constant vomiting does not cause weight loss!

Your body learns to adjust, and will start to digest the food slower, which means that when you throw up, the food may be 24 hours old, rather than the food you just ate! The stomach acids will also start to damage your teeth.

The best and only sensible way of controlling your weight is to "eat healthy meals and exercise regularly", and of course this is easy to say, but not necessarily easy to do.

Also look at the portions that you eat. Cut the size of portions that you put on your plate. We all have a natural tendency to eat whatever is put on our plate – part of our upbringing, but if you cut down the portions on your plate, you will find it easier to cut down on the amount that you eat.

An effective way to do this is the buy a set of smaller plate sizes. This way when you fill your plate, you have the feeling of a big meal, but it will be smaller.

Chefs will tell you that you "eat with your eyes and then with your mouth".

From a dieting view, what this means is that if you surround yourself with sugary drinks and sweets, it is almost certain that you will eat them. To avoid these foods, surround yourself with fruits and vegetables instead, you will then only be tempted to eat these healthier options. The same applies to when you go to a supermarket. Avoid the bad food options when you 'buy' and they won't be tempting you back in your home.

If you have a problem, see a proper Dietician who will plan a diet especially for you. At least then you know what you should and shouldn't be eating.

While there are heaps of diets in magazines these may not be right for you.

A dietician can plan one exactly for you taking into account the foods you like and the things you don't. They will also understand what you are going through, without being judgmental or critical.

If you know you are using laxatives, or bingeing out on chocolate, then ban these from the house. If they are not in the cupboard, then by making them harder to get hold of, you will hopefully get over the need to have them.

Be strong. No one is the 'perfect weight', and boys won't drop at your feet if you have the 'perfect weight'. If they don't like you for who you are, then that's their tough luck. While teasing is more to do with the fun of trying to bait someone into reacting, than trying to be hurtful, if it is hurtful, then rather than insult the person back tell them that what they are saying is really hurting you and ask them to stop doing it. They may well be shocked by your very direct response and if it continues, drop them as a friend. Don't just accept it.

Friends can be very helpful. If you or your friends are suffering from Anorexia, Bulimia or Binge Eating, then talk about it openly. Don't hide it away or deny it. The more you bury the problem, the harder it will be to fix the problem.

Like all problems, talking about the problem is the release valve. The more you openly discuss the problem you have, the easier it will be for people to help you.

If they don't know you have a problem, or if you constantly deny that you have a problem, or tell the person to mind their own business, the harder it will be to solve the problems you have.

Anorexia and Bulimia are not problems that simply resolve themselves. They can reoccur, and they can last many years, and affect not only you, but also the people around you.

Remember, you are not alone, and people are very willing to help.

Professional advice is also there for you, and there are also many internet services where you can talk about your problem, without having to directly meet people if you don't want to.

CHAPTER ELEVEN
PHONES, BULLIES, SOCIAL MEDIA

When you were at school you probably learned about the 'Industrial Revolution' in the 19th century, when machines replaced people doing jobs. In turn cars, trains and trucks replaced horses and wagons and now we are looking at electric and driverless cars replacing cars running on gasoline and smart phones, plastic credit, debit cards, and cryptocurrency replacing the bank notes and coins that we have all used for centuries.

There has always been change in people's lives and today the smart phone has meant that everyone is connected by voice, texting, photos and videos. This is all amazing technology.

As with all things in life there are 'positive' and 'negative' values in having and using a smart phone.

The smart phone makes it easy to connect and keep in contact with friends, pay for things we want to buy, but then being easy, this makes it easier to spend than to save. Swiping your phone at a sales counter feels a less like parting with real money!

Smart phones have also enabled many apps and social media too.

Everyone loves 'social media' where we can connect with friends, but we can also ignore a request to become a friend or block or unfriend a person too.

For most people this 'power' is a way to control who they are connected to and this all makes good sense. At the same time there are those people who abuse this power and this has given rise to the 'cyberbully' and 'trolls'.

At school you no doubt saw the development of small 'cliques' – the 'in crowd' – who excluded those who 'didn't fit' and sometimes would go out of their way to bully or intimidate others.

The smart phone has given these people more power – so they can send messages, photos and insults at any time of the day from wherever they are located. They can work as one person or as a group.

If you're on the receiving end of this abuse, insults or other horrible texts or emails, it can be very hurtful. The 'abusers' and trolls also know this. They are setting out to hit out at your weakest points. They will tell you 'gossip', that a friend has said this or that, giving weight to what they are saying and telling you as many lies as they can to make sure they hurt you as much as possible.

It is also easy to then hit back with an email or text back at them but the more you respond, the more they will love it.

The only way to stop them is to de-friend them straight away and not communicate. They will also still try and get to you via other friends of yours. You need to be strong and if the taunts get to be bad, tell your mother or father or someone in authority what is happening and turn off your phone. In certain situations, police can also be involved in stopping the trolls.

Abusive people have problems themselves and they love to dominate others as a way of making themselves seem important. You might really want to respond, and you can, but why would you bother with communicating with someone who wants to abuse you?

You can intimidate them more by being silent and ignoring them.

In this situation, silence is the best response. The more you engage with them the worse it will be.

In most cases they will be trying to make lies sound like the truth and making up gossip related to what someone said or did. Don't believe everything that you hear! If someone did say 'something' go back to the source and ask them if they did. Then determine whether they are telling the truth or lying too.

A lot of trolls are bold on-line, but weak if you talk directly with them.

CHAPTER TWELVE
LEARNING TO SMOKE

To light up or not to light up …

If you have grown up in a household where one or both of your parents are smokers, you will know all about the cost of smoking cigarettes and about the effects it has on people's health with the lingering smell of cigarettes in your clothes and hair.

Health warnings have been given in relation to smoking for decades, and in most western societies, cigarette advertising has been banned for years, so why do people smoke?

Smokers know that cigarettes are bad for their health, yet they continue to smoke regardless of the risks. Vaping also has unknown risks too, so why would you vape?

You are probably aware that cigarettes and some vapes contain nicotine, which is highly addictive. Very simply what this means is that once you have smoked cigarettes over time, it will become more and more difficult for you to break the habit because your body has developed a need for the nicotine.

The nicotine craving makes it hard for people to break the habit, but there are nicotine patches sold that provide a low level of nicotine through the skin, rather than though a cigarette. These patches are designed to help you break the craving. There are also e-cigarettes and other medications available too.

In order to be successful, smokers and vapers must really *want* to break the habit. It doesn't happen by itself. It takes discipline and a commitment.

You also know that in most societies, they are banning smoking, e-cigarettes and vaping on airlines, in restaurants, buses, trains, workplaces, bars and virtually anywhere where people are likely to light up.

So, knowing that cigarettes are expensive to buy – a packet a day will cost say $10 +, which multiplied by 364 days equals $ 3640 a year. Cigarettes are clearly addictive and bad for your health, so why do people continue to smoke, particularly in some countries a pack can cost around $40! Do the math!

Firstly, people do not see people dying in the streets when they light up! Dying from the effects of cigarettes can be very, very slow, but there is no disputing the fact that cigarettes will cause health problems at some point, increasing your risk of cancer, heart disease and other health problems.

Sure, there are people who have smoked cigarettes their entire life and are still living at 90 years old, and there are also people who have never smoked a cigarette in their life who have dropped dead in their twenties.

Smoking traditionally was marketed to convey sophistication and worldliness. Film stars all smoked, and it was a way for a man to prove he was tough and strong, and for a woman to show her independence. "The Marlboro Man" – tough, rugged and handsome, and "the sophisticated, international world of Peter Stuyvesant".

It was very grown up, and for teenagers it was a way that they could show to everyone who was looking that they were very grown up too! They were independent of their parents, carrying their own money, and 'really cool' - part of the in crowd.

This desire to 'make a statement', to show off, and prove to the world at large that we are independent, and all grown up is very definitely one of the main reasons why people smoke. The cigarette therefore becomes a symbol of this, a sign of strength and resolve.

Smokers also like to have a cigarette in their fingers.

If you watch a smoker, they will put the cigarette to their lips, and draw the smoke in, but they will more than likely hold it in their fingers most of the time. It is a means of 'having something to do with their fingers and hands', and without it they tend to fidget.

Cigarettes also become a friend. They take on the role of a dependable constant in the smoker's life. This is one of the reasons why people stay on one brand, rather than try all sorts of brands. By and large, smokers are very loyal to the brand that they smoke, although cost of cigarettes can get them to trade down to cheaper brands.

As a "friend", their cigarettes are always there for them, and like a good friend, they allow the person to take a few minutes break from whatever they are doing. A cigarette break therefore becomes a form of relaxation.

Cigarette smokers will also often associate the good times they have had, with times that they are smoking, so it also becomes emotionally hard to break the habit. Many smokers also form the opinion that they can control their weight by smoking, and if they stop smoking, they will immediately put on lots of weight. It is very hard to break the habit, but people can do it.

Emotionally, men will tend to smoke to relieve tension and stress. They will arrive early for an appointment and have a quick smoke before they go into the meeting or will light up while they are waiting for people to turn up, so that they are not alone.

They can be seen to be having a cigarette, as opposed to standing alone with no apparent reason! For women, they tend to smoke more when they are happy, as a means of relaxing, or as a small celebration of comfort and composure.

Cigarettes will also bring people together, as a means of having a conversation, while they share a cigarette together. In a fast-moving world, a little time out is always a bonus.

Trouble is the places where this is possible are getting fewer, and there are a lot of people committed to 'hating cigarette smokers', and their "dirty habit".

If you want to quit smoking and don't have the willpower, then see a pharmacist in a drug store for medications, or your doctor, or phone a Quit line. There are lots of Government organizations to help, as well as everyone from Hypnotists to Herbalists.

One way of quitting is to wrap a plastic band around the pack. This means that every time you take a cigarette you become conscious of doing it, so you are not smoking just out of habit!

So, do you need to smoke? If you don't need a psychological crutch that a cigarette provides and would prefer the smell of clean air to the smell of cigarettes in your clothes and hair, then bank the money you save and congratulate yourself. If you don't start smoking, you won't have to quit.

CHAPTER THIRTEEN
BUYING A CAR

Your first big purchase!

So, you would love a Porsche and maybe a Ferrari!

So, buy one!

Buy a miniature one that is that you can put in your bedroom and keep your dreams alive! It won't cost you much money, will be cheap to run, and you won't have to pay for insurance.

It's the best sort of car, because every other car will cost you lots of money, either in the purchase or in running expenses - petrol, tires, repairs, insurance, and whatever you paid for it. Also, when it comes to selling the car, most likely you will sell it for less than you bought it for, so again another cost.

No matter what sort of car you buy, it will cost you money, but so too will catching the bus!

For most people, having a car is freedom. It allows you to go wherever the road takes you, to stop and go when you want to without a timetable. You can travel alone, or with friends, carry whatever you want, have the music loud, and do pretty much whatever you want. It's your car, and it's your space, your own piece of privacy.

So, how do decide what sort of car to buy?

With a huge choice of autos available, and lots of people ready to sell you the first auto you see, you will find the best "high pressure salespeople" in the world ready to help you "do a deal".

Before even looking at any cars, you must first decide how much money you want to spend and try and stick to your budget.

The purchase of a car comes down to a series of decisions. Remember how we talked about decisions earlier?

Firstly, how much money do you have?

When the salesman or salesperson sells you a car, they will be trying to sell you two things - one, the car and two, the finance. They will make money on the car as a commission and they will also make a commission on the finance package, and maybe even the insurance policy too!

If you don't have enough money, they will want you to go into debt.

Debt was once something that people tried to avoid at all costs, but today, money is often available very easily, and debt enables you to buy things that you normally couldn't afford.

Can you afford to have a debt? The answer is easy. How easy can you pay it off? This introduces the notion of cashflow. Cashflow is the amount of money that is coming into your pocket, relative to the amount of money going out, and in finance, be it on an individual level or in a business, cashflow is critical.

If more money is going out than coming in, or some of this money is at risk, meaning may not happen, then you have what is called a negative cashflow, which could in fact become more negative if the income you were hoping for didn't happen.

What you need is positive cashflow - ie more money coming in then going out, ideally what accountants like to call creating a 'surplus'.

When looking at your own cashflow, you need to make judgments on the expenses you have prior to buying a car, and after. This way you can work out what you can afford to pay out each week, and how much you can afford to repay on a loan. If you don't have to go into debt, don't do it, but also don't be afraid of debt.

Debt is no problem if you have the cashflow to support it and is even less of a problem if you are using that money to make more money than the money is costing you - more about this later.

Working out what your income is easy. Your expenses however are harder to work out, as we all think that we have our expenses are much smaller than they are. Where does your money go?

Break your expenses into regular payments and then irregular ones, and then look at your cash surplus. This amount will tell you what you can afford to pay out/borrow and what you can't or shouldn't.

Remember too, that a car could also cost you unplanned expenses. Also add these into your budget.

So, now that you have worked out what you can afford, and what you can't, you're ready to buy your first car.

What do you buy? How do you decide? Should you buy a new car or a second hand one?

If you buy a new car it will come with a warranty – but of course it will be more expensive than a second hand one. Even so, once the new car is driven for even a few miles, it will depreciate (go down in value) so some of the best value cars to buy are ones that have a low mileage. They may

also come with a warranty too. An auto dealer may well have both new car sales people and used vehicle sales people, both selling on commission. Before you buy the low mileage auto, check the new car price too. Sometimes the used price may be higher than the new auto price!

Most times it is better to buy a car brand and model that is popular as being 'popular' also suggests that other people have had a good experience with that brand of car and model. Also pick a color that you think is popular too.

Buying an older car is a riskier choice but a cheap price doesn't always mean it is likely to break down. It could of course happen and that's the risk you take, but it also means that you are not making payments every month on financing a new car or paying full comprehensive insurance. 3rd Party property insurance covers damage costs of a car that you run into, but not your own. Comprehensive insurance covers both your car and the other car. Note however that Insurance Policies come with an 'excess' – eg $600 excess or higher, meaning that you will have to pay the first $600 of any damage that occurs.

While it may cost you more, the newer the car you purchase the more likely it is to not cost you money in repairs when you drive it away, but it will go down in value regardless.

If a car has obvious defects, it will absolutely have ones that are not obvious, and these are the ones that will cost you the big bucks! Give it a big miss, even if it is cheap. Also think about your safety. A bigger car has more metal in it. This generally should mean that it is has more inbuilt protection than a smaller car. Generally, but not always! The bigger car will also cost you more to run in fuel – and every week you will need to fill the car up with fuel – all cash out!

Don't get hooked on a car just because it has a great sound system, or the color is right. There are always more cars around the corner at other yards, so don't make your decision too fast. Sleep on it! It's always far easier to buy, than it is to sell.

Sometimes the hardest decision is to say "No".

Sure, you don't want to hurt someone's feelings, or feel you might lose the deal, but the sales person knows that he or she have a big chance of losing the sale if you say "No, I'll think about it", or "I would like to get a mechanic to check it over", or "my friend to look at it". They want you to sign for it now, and they will put doubts and pressure on you to see if you will jump into the deal straight away. They want the sale.

They may also tell small lies – the main one being that there is someone else looking at the car, and they are due to make a decision later that same day! Your natural reaction is that you want to beat them to the great deal, but is it really true that there was another buyer?

Get someone who knows about cars to look at it, but ultimately it will be your decision as to whether you buy or not.

Do you feel comfortable in it? Do you like the car itself? Never simply buy because someone told you that it was the right thing to do. It is your decision, and you must feel comfortable with the decision you make.

Also look at the yard where you are buying the car. What is the general quality of cars in the yard? If they are all bombs, chances are yours will be too! A dealer in bombs can only make money if they minimize their expenditure, meaning don't do repairs, don't give you warranties, and don't fix any defects that you find after you've bought the car.

It is always better to go to a better dealer, and pay more to get a better car, with better after sales service. The biggest cost is the purchase, and what value you will lose once you drive it away, and it is easy to spend a whole lot on repairs, with not much to show for that money spent.

Just as there are good dealers and bad, there are also good cars and bad. Every manufacturer has brought out models of cars that are duds for one reason or another. To avoid buying a dud, ask around to find out which models are better than others.

Once you have decided on a brand of car ask a mechanic in a workshop if the model you are thinking of purchasing is good or not, and if there are any problems with the model. They won't be trying to sell you a car, therefore will hopefully give you a more truthful answer.

As per above, even if you are looking at second hand cars, also look at new ones. Sometimes a new car can be cheaper than a second hand one because of a special manufacturer deal at the time. Don't assume that a second-hand car will be cheaper than the same new model. There are new car dealers and second-hand dealers – with different deals happening so it could well be one has better deals than the other.

A new car will also come with a manufacturer's warranty – which may be parts only, or parts and labor too - maybe for twelve months, or even seven years. The longer it is, and the more it covers the better, as it means that you won't have to pay for repairs should they happen. Note labor costs are usually much more than parts, so check to see if the warranty covers parts only, or parts and labor.

With Finance there are all sorts of things to watch out for. With Finance packages, what they are selling you is money! Note the word 'selling', because there are lots of tricks to suck you in! These are a few of them – "interest free for the first 12 months" sounds good, until you see the interest after the interest free period – eg 24.4 %; " No deposit terms" – means the Finance company will own the car, and you will be locked into a contract at probably a very high interest; "weekly Payments" – deliberately sets out to show you a low figure, to emphasize how affordable the loan is! You might be scared off by the monthly figure!!

Also check the small print. Sometimes interest rates may be simple, or maybe compound interest, meaning that if you borrowed $10,000 and had paid out $9000 of this loan, you could be still paying interest on the original $10,000.

Often Finance companies will quote a variable rate – meaning it will rise and fall as rates change ie start at 9.9% but could rise to 14%, or they won't quote any rate, simply a repayment schedule. They will also add the interest straight onto your loan when you take it out ie Borrow $10,000, could mean that you immediately owe $11,000 (10%), or higher and the repayments will be made on that basis.

The trick is always to shop around for the best deal for you. A lower interest rate can make a big difference to the cost of the loan. Banks lend money, as do Credit Unions and heaps of other places, even your parents – who may even give you a good rate if you're nice to them!!

In getting Finance, you may also be asked for a "guarantor" – meaning a person who will guarantee that your repayments will be met. This may be a parent or another person who agrees to be bound by the contract. If you are the guarantor for someone, and they default (ie don't pay) you will be the one liable for the debt! Think very carefully about being a guarantor, even if you are asked.

The next thing you need is insurance. To get insurance, phone around different insurance companies to get a quote for the car you are wishing to purchase. Quotes will vary, and sometimes, some car models will have such a high premium, that it will put you off buying the car. As a new driver, you will be paying the top premium because of your age – and some companies won't even insure drivers under 25.

What the insurance company is doing is charging you a higher premium, because of the higher risk attached to new drivers in your age group, and the risk of theft.

They may also say that you will have to pay for the first $600 excess or more of any claim you make. This excess amount will vary from company to company. Every time you claim, you may have to pay a higher premium, losing your no claim bonus (so-called). The insurance company makes money out of you paying money to them, not the other way around, so they are trying to discourage you from claiming!

They will also have statements saying that they will not pay if the driver is under the influence of alcohol or drugs. If you were to be in an accident and drunk, you would also be responsible for the cost of the damage, not the insurance company!

Never ever, repeat, never ever drive your car without having insurance, and particularly check, if you drive someone else's car, make sure that they are covered with comprehensive insurance and that you trust what they tell you. 'Comprehensive' insurance means that both the car you are driving, and the one that you might run into are both covered!

'Third party' **property** insurance simply means that the other car is covered, not the one you're driving! So, if your friend's car is damaged by you, or stolen while it is in your care, and the car is not covered, you will be the one paying! Even worse however is if they don't have insurance, and you run into a new luxury car. You could well be paying for the damage for the next ten years.

You may well ask if the owner of the car has insurance, and they say 'Yes', but neglect to tell you that they only have third party insurance, or that their insurance doesn't cover young drivers. Be aware, and preferably don't drive other people's cars.

In most countries it is compulsory to have Third party <u>Personal</u> cover, (don't confuse this with <u>property</u> cover), as part of the Car's Registration. Third party personal cover protects you from claims made by <u>people</u> hurt as a result of an accident.

Your first car purchase is an exciting one and will be a purchase that you will remember for a long time. Hopefully it is a good purchase, one where you love the car, the freedom it gives you, and the places you get to drive to.

CHAPTER FOURTEEN
SAVING MONEY

How do you do that?

Let's face it, saving money is not easy, and no matter what your age, it doesn't necessarily get any easier. However, there are some tricks to saving that may help you.

As an adult, you will be in control of your own money; how you earn it; how you spend it; and how you either let it flow through your fingers, save or invest it. One way or another you have already been involved with money throughout your life, but now you will be starting to earn it yourself, pay your bills and spend it. Spending is the fun bit, and everyone loves to do it! It is also far easier to spend than to save!

There is a saying that "Money burns a hole in your pocket". What this means is that having the money in your pocket creates almost a 'craving' to spend it. Do an experiment – walk through a shopping center with $100 in your pocket and see how much you have left by the time you leave. Now do the same experiment with only coins in your pocket and then see how much you spend.

Most people will splurge their money on the day they get paid, and then just before the next payday, they become totally frugal, counting every cent to make sure it lasts the distance.

Remember the story of the three little pigs? How one built a house of straw, one of sticks and one of bricks? This story had a very clear message about life in it, and the story hasn't changed in a thousand years.

Sure, everyone wants to be the smart little pig! To take the time to build a strong house; a secure future; have money in the bank and a good career, but it won't happen to all of us, and even the smartest little pig will make mistakes.

There's a common saying that "money doesn't grow on trees".

Yet, look at how many fortunes have been made from trees - from timber, building, transport, paper, paper products, printing on paper, recycling paper and the use of paper, sap, resins, rubber, bark, fragrances, as well as from selling trees, plants, flowers, timber to build with, and of course landscaping and real estate.

It is a question of what you see, and what others don't.

This is often the way that fortunes are made.

I remember meeting a man who told me that he had worked in underground mines. He collected all the rubbish – the used metal, timber, and so on. Each day as he went into the mine, the team of miners coming out would tease him about the work he was doing picking up the rubbish– yet he was making more money than the whole team combined! The point is, what is rubbish to one person is gold to another!

It used to be that the main way of saving money was to put it in the bank.

These days the bank term "savings account" is probably a misnomer, because with bank fees and charges you are *paying* the bank to hold your funds for the convenience of the bank service. To be able to withdraw money anywhere in the world from an ATM Automatic Teller Machine is a truly amazing service, as is being able to use a plastic card as money!

You need to therefore adjust your thinking. Stop thinking that "bank interest" is important when it comes to saving. The facts tell you that banks are trying to get your money for nothing, and make you pay for the service they provide.

So, think of banks as a service that you pay for.

As a service, they have a very good one, given that you can transfer funds around the world, withdraw money virtually anywhere, use plastic cards for credit, direct debits and walk into almost any business and pay for the transaction using your phone or a piece of plastic. The most important service they provide are loans.

By borrowing money, you are hopefully able to buy something that you normally couldn't afford, or maybe invest what you have borrowed into something that will give you a bigger return!

This great service is however a great temptation to spend money! It's just so easy!

There's a very simple way to save money, and that is not to spend it.

Dead easy, right? No, of course it's not.

Firstly, try to work out what sort of spender you are. Do you always want the latest 'name' clothing, CD's, or takeaway food or do you always look for the cheapest item? Do you shop around, or just buy when you see something you like? Would you always catch a taxi, or prefer to walk if you need to travel somewhere? Are you more likely to spend $100 if it's in your wallet or bag, than you would if you only have $15 in cash with you?

What is the main "spending attraction" for you? Can you walk straight past a cosmetic counter, phone store, jewelry shop or clothing rack without stopping, or picking something up? How strong are you to resist?

Do you really care if you do or don't spend money? Do you blow your money every Friday night at the pub?

If you just can't help yourself, then you now know what you need to resist! If having money in your pocket makes you want to spend it, don't carry so much money. If you are always tempted to spend in clothing stores, stay away from them as much as possible. It may be hard, but you are the only one in control of what you do, and what you spend.

When you get paid, try to hang out as long as you possibly can before spending, until the excitement of your first pay check has diminished. Some people think their pay check is like winning the lottery, so they go on spending spree. Resist the temptation, at least for a few days. Even not spending for one or two days will make a big difference to how much you spend or save in a fortnight. The worst thing you can do is to spend all your money *before* you get you receive your next pay check.

One trick is to have two separate bank accounts- one that is very accessible, and one that is not.

By running two bank accounts you are clearly separating your finances into two bundles - one that you can spend from (note you don't have to spend it all), and one that you don't spend from. This may seem incredibly simple and it is, but it also works. Once you have done this you will find that your savings will go up, and you will spend less. It becomes a psychological barrier to stop you spending, and it will become a reason for saving. Choose the savings account carefully however to ensure that you don't just run up fees at the bank! You can also automate the payments from your pay or main account to your savings account.

Another simple plan is to set an objective or target that you want to achieve - say $1000 or $2000. Work out the number of months you want to take to get to this nominated amount, and then go for it.

Different budget plans will work for different people. Most people don't have any plan, so if you have a plan, at least you are in advance of most.

To understand money, you need to understand some very basic concepts about money.

The first is that money, meaning dollars and cents, rupees, euros, yen, or other currency is the currency of a country, and that currency is the means to conduct exchange of goods and services. At one time gold and silver were the means of exchange, but they were so heavy that it was better to break them down into at first gold and silver coins, and then later notes made of paper or plastic, a form of IOU (I owe you).

It is only in the late 1990's that most countries abandoned the idea of using Gold as a standard measure of exchange. A lot of gold that was stored in the treasury departments or central banks was then sold off on the open market, for use in jewelry and general use, rather than being used as a means of exchange.

While some countries have fixed exchange rates, others float their currency, meaning that they allow their currency to rise and fall in relation to demand for their currency. Exchange rates are quoted each day in the press.

Others looking for currency stability, may even opt to use United States dollars as their currency, while in most of Europe they have a single European currency, the Euro. Having one currency minimizes the need to change the currency every time you cross a border within most of Europe.

So, how does this affect you?

In one sense it doesn't, other than if you travel, but the main point to understand is that currency, cash or money is like all other products - it has a price, a demand, and it is the most 'liquid' of all assets. All other assets are judged in relation the speed with which they can be converted to cash – how liquid they are.

If you own a TV or a car, it will have a value, but that value will rise or fall, depending on how saleable or non-salable it is. Its true value can only be determined when it is converted to cash. The *speed* that an asset can be converted to cash, is a measure of its *liquidity value*. Shares are more liquid than real estate property, simply because they can be converted to cash within days of selling them.

As much as we all want cash, holding cash is no way to build it up. You have to convert it into assets and for those assets to *grow* in value, not decline in value. Very simply, what this means is buying something for $1 and selling it for more than $1.

If I put $100 in the bank, they will take out bank charges or fees. If you were able to get 6% PA (per annum) interest, then at the end of one year, theoretically you would have $106. Not much you say, and you're right.

Remember that interest payments can be calculated daily, on a minimum monthly basis, yearly or as simple interest or compound interest. Each will give a different value.

Most banks may also have fees or bank charges on their accounts, meaning that instead of earning $6.00 dollars in interest on your $100, you may get a fee instead (eg $10) that means that your $100 deposited for the year (12 Months) is now $96 dollars.

If you could buy something for $1 and at the end of the year sell it, meaning convert it back to cash for $2, then you will have doubled your money - a 100% return but it took 12 months to do it, but it is still better than the $100 dollar example above.

Compare now the returns if you were able to reinvest your money each month and double your money each time. On the first month you would have $2, on the second month the $2 would become $4, third month $8, fourth month $16 and by the end of the 12 months, believe it or not, you would have $4096 in cash!

Sounds easy, doesn't it, but with each transaction it becomes harder to do. What I have shown here is what happens when you have both been able to double your money every month and convert back to cash on every transaction.

What happens if on the 12th month if you can't convert back to cash? This would mean that you would have to discount the sale to find a buyer. At the end of the eleventh month you have $2048 in cash, so as long as you are able to get more than this amount you are still way ahead of where you would have been if you had simply left the money in the bank.

The three points to take out of this example are firstly that the ability to convert an asset back to cash is most important(liquidity); secondly that the more times the cash turns over is critical (turnover), and thirdly the higher the percentage increase then the more money you make.

The most critical factor in all of this is the actual assets you buy.

With your $1 you could have bought an ice cream, which at the time you thought of it as an asset. If you ate it, then the asset is gone, in which case the $1 is gone too!

In contrast, you could have sold the ice cream to someone else for $2, therefore doubling the value of the asset. What you do with the asset is therefore critical.

As much as these examples are pure theory, the reality is pretty much the same. The difficulty is finding the assets that will give you this sort of return.

Assets can be very variable. You can invest in ice creams, stocks and shares, property, cars, or a thousand other things. The greatest thing to invest in is however yourself, and your judgment of what you believe will give you the best returns.

As soon as you buy anything, you are investing - be it buying a TV, a guitar, a computer, clothing or surfboard. Most of these 'investments (assets) won't give you any investment return and in most cases you will lose money when you eventually convert them to cash, assuming that you were able to do that.

Even though most of these assets will go down in value, they are still assets, and as you buy more substantial ones such as computers, cars, TV's etc, and you either pay them off, or own them outright, then you will start to see that your 'assets' are now on paper starting to have a real value. You should be proud of doing that. It is a real achievement.

While something like 93% of people find it hard to save, a lot of people find it far easier to pay things off. It becomes a commitment, which they know that they must meet or risk defaulting. Paying things off, so long as you are committed to paying them off, is sometimes a better way to gain assets, then trying to commit to saving first, and then purchasing later on. This really comes down to assessing your own needs and ability to being careful in the way that you spend.

If you are in a unit or flat sharing, you can probably get away with owning no furniture, and just your clothes, but you could also start to buy your own furniture – furniture that you really like, which will retain at least some of its value.

Having a good bed, or a good TV, computer or Sound System will make you feel good, simply because you own it, giving you a sense of achievement and self esteem. Plus, you get to enjoy it everyday, rather than putting up with an old bed, or small TV. The same applies to a car or computer.

When it comes time to buy something big where you have to borrow from a bank or other lender, they will be asking you to do an 'Assets and Liabilities Statement', which means a table showing what you own, and what you owe to other people.

Typically, this will look something like this

Assets (what you own)		Liabilities (what you owe)	
Cash in bank	$ 2500	Credit Card	$ 400
Furniture	$ 1500		
Car	$ 6000	Car loan	$ 2600
Rental Bond	$ 900		
Total	$ 10,900		$ 3000
Balance	$ 7900		

Congratulate yourself if you have more assets than liabilities and if you don't then work towards achieving it. Having money in the bank is like a security blanket! It will help you to relax.

In contrast, having no money, or not enough to make your payments on the car or TV, is what is called 'Financial Stress', and this type of stress can be devastating to you and everyone else who depend on you.

You should try to avoid putting yourself in this position, and certainly the bank lender is wanting to make sure that you are not stretching yourself too far when you apply for a loan. Be aware, that some lenders couldn't care whether you defaulted or not. This is particularly when they are being paid a commission on the 'sale', which is what you are to them.

There is a Latin legal term called 'caveat emptor', which means 'buyer beware'. In other words, it is up to you to be aware that you are being sold something, and up to you to determine that it is a fair and reasonable offer, <u>not</u> the seller looking after their own interests!

Some lenders will only lend money on the basis of how much income and equity you have (the amount of your own money you own in a car or a property) versus what you are borrowing eg a 60% equity. Others will lend up to 105% or more, but beware, if you do default for any reason, you have no equity to fall back on.

They may also ask you or someone you know to go 'Guarantor' for the loan. This means that if the person defaults, that the guarantor will pay the full amount of the outstanding debt – as we pointed out in an earlier chapter.

Never go guarantor, just to help a friend! If your friend disappears, you may well have a debt that you didn't expect, and this situation is not uncommon.

The lender may ask for a monthly *cash flow* statement from you to see where your money is going and look to judge how *secure* your income is. This is usually determined by things such as the amount of time you have spent at a home address, and how long you have worked at a particular organization. The more you can demonstrate 'stability' the better they like it.

If your income is $500 per week, but you need to pay out $100 for rent, $60 for transport, and $80 on a personal loan, then you have $260 in uncommitted funds. Alas, you have to eat and want to go out - an amount that you will need to estimate. You will also need to show how much you are likely to be able to save each week. Can you afford the loan? The lender will look at these figures, and then ask to see your bank statement to verify that what you have said is reflected through your bank balance. If all looks good, and you have a clear surplus each week, it probably means that you can afford to borrow and repay the loan!

By borrowing and then repaying your loan, you are building up a 'credit rating'. All lenders will do what they call a 'credit check' on you to see if there are any outstanding or bad debts (meaning unpaid) in your name. If you have never borrowed any money, then there will be no record, and this often means that they won't lend because you have no track record!

By borrowing and repaying loans, you are building up your credit rating! Building up a bad record however can be disastrous, as your bad credit rating may well last for years and is often hard to get around, even if your circumstances have changed.

There is also a question of timing. There are good times to borrow and bad times. It is essentially easier to borrow money than it is to repay it. It is also easier to spend than to save, so what you must be very sure of is your cash flow when you borrow, meaning sure that you have allowed for any and all possibilities when you borrow.

If you are not sure you want to stay in the job you have, don't borrow until you are so. If you are likely to have some big bills coming up, try to pay them first before you borrow.

There is a definite *psychology* to money too, both on an individual and total economy level. People talk about the economy going into recession or coming out of it or predicting that there will be a boom or bust next year or the year after, and while some of these predictions will be based on trends, the biggest factor of all is what people are *feeling* in relation to these predictions.

There is the world economy, the country's economy, local economy and your own economy – which is the most important one for you.

If people feel good, feel confident, they are more likely to spend. If they are not, they will generally stop spending. The *psychological attitude towards money*, and the financial situation at the time, will have much greater influence than the facts - whatever they are, will or won't be. Much of this psychology about money will be based on what people hear or read in the newspapers or on TV, and there will never be a total logic as to why or why not people react the way they do. It may be easy enough to rationalize the logic, but logical it isn't!

There are many people who do better in a recession then they do in boom times, and vice versa. There are financial trends that are predictable, but also many which are not. You as an individual can react changing your behavior each time something changes, or you can ride over these obstacles, plotting your own course, rather than changing to fit others.

When the Captain of the USS Missouri steaming down the coast sighted a 'blip' on his radar screen directly ahead, he signaled ahead... "This is the USS Missouri. Please alter course to avoid contact". The blip replied "Message received. Please alter your course to avoid collision". The Captain was highly indignant to receive this message and replied in the sternest possible way – "This is the Captain of the USS Missouri, the biggest aircraft carrier in the US Navy. Please identify yourself, and I repeat, please alter course immediately to avoid collision".

The reply came back "Please alter your course to avoid collision. This is the Fort Danger Lighthouse. We are unable to alter our course!"

So, what position will you take? Will you alter your course, or plot your own?

Credit is very easy to obtain in most cases, with banks delighted to give you a credit card, and regularly upgrade the limit that you have based on you paying the minimum payment each month. Credit cards have very high interest rates, and banks make a fortune out of them.

If you pay just the minimum payments each month, they will be making great money from you, but you will be getting deeper in debt each month as well. Credit cards should really be called debt cards – and debt is debt.

These days it is almost impossible not to have credit cards as in many situations you may need a credit card or debit card to make a purchase.

Having two or more cards however should be recognized as risky as it makes it very easy to spend unless you are very disciplined.

Just look at your credit card statement and see what is highlighted by the bank and what is not.

In almost all cases the interest rate is hidden or downplayed, and they will highlight the minimum payment, but not what you owe. Reason – they want to keep you in debt. The banks are not your friend.

At an interest rate of 20%, when you don't make a purchase using your credit card, think of it as making 20% on the money you didn't spend! Also, by having only one credit card, you are also creating a savings plan – by not spending more than you can reasonably pay off.

In the same way, phone companies will sell you a phone on a plan, with $0 to pay up front. It is only when you look at the fine print that you see that you have signed up for a two-year contract with built in repayments every month for a phone that they have sold you worth hundreds if not more than a thousand dollars!

There are lots of traps in finance, and they are not all easy to pick, so be careful. Believe it or not, there are many teenagers who have run up hundreds of dollars on mobile phones and committed suicide because of the debt and related stress that it has caused. No phone is worth that.

By now you will have worked out that you will never make your fortune simply by saving money and putting it in a bank savings account and being frugal in your spending. But then, what should you invest in?

Earlier we said the best investment is in yourself and this is true. That means in most cases establishing a secure career that you enjoy and that pays well. By paying well, you will gain a regular pay packet and be able to build up surplus money that you could invest and not spend.

Most fortunes come from investment in business, property and stock and shares, not from working for a wage or salary.

These investments all involve risk in one form or another and the higher the risk the less secure the investment.

The first question to ask yourself is how much money do you have to invest? This will determine what you can realistically invest in.

What you are looking for is the ROI – return on investment, but as a young adult with limited money, there will be investments that are possible and ones that are not. For example, it is unlikely that you will be able to finance purchase of an iron ore mine or high-rise building, even though there may be great returns on that investment. The same may be true of trying to buy a house or unit.

What you can do however is to buy shares in a company that has an Iron ore mine or owns property and there are thousands of companies that are listed on the stock exchange where you could invest as little as a hundred dollars.

Would you be prepared to invest 100 or 500 hundred dollars, knowing that you run the risk of losing some or even all of that money?

Shares go up but also down in value and there is an old saying that "You should not invest in shares if you are not prepared to lose it (the money)". There are also counter arguments to this to say that "Paper loses are only real losses when you sell".

Countless books have been written on share trading, charting, technical analysis, trends, bull and bear markets and it is impossible to cover all of this in a few short words. It is however worth building up at least some knowledge of how investors, day traders, brokers, new listings, capital raisings, financial markets all work and there are lots of resources available to enable you to build up your knowledge base.

Here is a brief outline of some of the terms you might see or read about –

Ticker – this is the Stock Exchange code for the stock eg Tesla Ticker is TSLA as listed on the Nasdaq exchange

Market Cap (Capitalization) the Total $ value of the company at that time.

Last Sale – the share price when last traded yesterday when the market closed for the day.

Highs and Lows – the highest and lowest price of the stock in the last day, week, month, year to date or last 12 months.

Dividend Yield – the Annual last dividend based on today's share price. Note: many shares don't earn or profit or pay a dividend.

P/E Ratio (Price/earnings) ratio of the share price based on *projected* earnings. Not necessarily actual earnings. A high PE number suggests high expectations of growth.

Charts –all chart forms are designed to show trends – from line charts over different periods of time, to bar charts, comparative ones, candlesticks, Stochastic, moving average and others.

Market segments – stocks fall into different industry sectors – eg Mining, Technology, Financial, Agricultural etc.

Growth Stocks – Shares that suggest the company is growing

Revenue Stocks – shares that pay a regular dividend yield.

Speculative stocks – shares that are higher risk but with big hopes for success in finding their fortune

Day traders – are people who buy and sell shares every day as a business

Long term Investors – people who buy shares and just hold on to them for the growth in their stock price or for the Dividend that the shares pay out.

Picking the Top or Bottom of a share price – to capitalize on the changes in the price of the stock.

New Listing – It costs a lot of money to list on a Stock Exchange and to fulfill all the on-going regulative costs. New companies 'list' and their stock value will then go up or down based on the information they inform the market with.

Averaging down – means that if you own shares in a company and the shares go down in value, you buy more, so that your overall purchase price is lower.

Share Portfolio – is the group of shares that you own.

Diversifying your portfolio – means investing in different shares and business sectors to spread your risk, so that if one share value goes down, another may be going up.

Trailing Stop-Loss – is a way of locking in a price to sell the shares eg 10% below the share price, so that you limit potential losses.

Minimum parcel size- shares all have different values and each will have a minimum number of shares that you can purchase

My advice – learn more, read Financial news and dip your toe in the water.

If you can't afford a 10 or 20% deposit for buying real estate, you are essentially locked out of buying property, certainly in the short term, so investing in stocks and shares may be a worthwhile course to take.

Shares do go up and down and each time you risk the money you invest, but you will only lose the actual money when you sell. The great advantage of buying shares is that they can be sold today and your money back in your bank tomorrow.

If for example, you set aside $200 each month as your investment fund and each month you purchased some shares where you believe in the company's story, over time you will have build up a 'share portfolio' with a value. You can also cash out that portfolio (liquidate) to get cash back at any time.

If you do decide to buy shares – the process begins by finding a broker and filling out details on their application form to prove your identity and depositing funds into an account with them to enable you to buy and sell shares. Most brokers are on-line and there are numbers of brokers, often sending out newsletters and charging bigger or smaller brokerage charges for their service.

The decisions of course are yours to take, but the $200 investment each month could be spent on shoes, clothes or food. Which will give more satisfaction and value?

CHAPTER FIFTEEN
SUICIDE

Not just a youth problem…

One of the saddest facts in society today are the number of deaths from suicide.

What you may not realize is that there are more than twice the number of deaths resulting from suicide as there are deaths from car accidents, and this is pretty much the case in the UK, USA, Australia and other developed countries.

There are also more suicide deaths than murders and twice as many as there are from Aids.

For every suicide there are up to 20 attempts.

In the UK, while more females attempt suicide, males are 4 times more likely to die. The highest risk group are people in the medical profession and farmers, the reason being that Doctors, Vets and nurses have more access to poisons, and farmers to guns.

In the USA some 58% of suicides used guns to kill themselves, and like the UK, men outnumber women 4 to 1 in the number of deaths caused through suicide.

In Japan some 71% of suicide deaths are by men, usually middle aged, and largely due to financial problems.

The number one reason for suicide throughout the world is depression, followed by alcohol abuse, drug usage and the combination of aggression and depression caused by separation and divorce.

While in the USA there are a high number of suicides by men over the age of 85, largely due to deteriorating health, and the general frustration of old age. Almost all people who suicide are physically fine and in good health. It is their mental state at the time that is not.

As we have discussed in an earlier chapter, everyone suffers with depressions during their lifetime, and there is no absolute reason why we either go into a depression or come out of them.

People generally simply accept depression like headaches, as being just part of life. The times when you are depressed may be short or may go on for a long time, and some people suffer depression a lot of times, and others very rarely.

We all can feel sad, just as we can be happy, and at one time or another mentally thought about suicide and death, without doing anything more, just as we have also thought about 'what happens' if we were to die in a car crash or some other way.

As we discussed earlier, if you think of a depression as being like a valley, then you will recognize that you will eventually climb out of the valley. A depression, like a valley will never last forever. It may however get deeper, before you climb out of it.

If you were in a general state of depression, and then something really extra bad happens, such as a death in the family, your parents breaking up, huge angry fights breaking out at home, your girlfriend telling you that she is dumping you, or you have just been told how useless and disgusting you are, then your depression may get deeper to the point where you cease to see the valley coming to an end, you simply see the 'pain of life' getting worse.

Someone bullying you physically or mentally even using text messaging can lead to depression too. If this happens, talk to someone else, or cut off the messenger and look for new friends who are outside of your current circle of friends. You need to break the cycle, not easy to do, but necessary.

With depression your whole world seems to have fallen apart, and all you want to do is end the pain! It is very easy to focus on all the bad things that have happened to you in life, without seeing any of the good times.

When pain like this happens, and pain like this *does* happen, you must find a way to reduce it, or increase your ability to cope.

If you broke your leg, you would know that you had to see a doctor, or if you cut yourself, you would bandage it up. Mental pain is just the same. You must do something about it.

As humans, our greatest means of stopping mental pain is by talking about it and by making ourselves as busy as possible to distract ourselves from the pain that is happening around us.

When you next watch the TV news and see a crime scene, think about how the firemen, police, ambulance or camera crews cope with what they are seeing. The thing is that they concentrate purely on the job they are doing, being as busy as possible and in so doing blocking out the emotional side of what they are seeing, as awful as that might be.

Being busy building something, playing a game, visiting people, working longer, even going to bed early, all distract us away from the pain we are directly seeing, hearing about or suffering.

It creates *time*, and *time* itself is a great healer, as is *talking*.

You must *deliberately* set out to break the mood.

Talking, even talking to a person who isn't listening, can be very helpful to you, as it allows you to express your feelings, and get it out of the debate between your 'inner' and 'outer' self, and the doubts that this may be creating. In hearing ourselves talk about our feelings, the problems we have, or the frustration, anger or aggression we have, helps *us* enormously.

Lots of people however find it very hard to talk. They would really prefer to keep their feelings to themselves, but in so doing they are creating even more pressure on themselves.

Sometimes it is far easier to talk to a stranger than it is to talk with people who know you, and there are lots of telephone services available, which are there for people who need to talk. This means that you can be anonymous. No-one knows who you are, but they are there to help people, and allow them to talk.

Just as you know that if you were to pump up a tire and keep pumping, that it would eventually burst as the pressure continues to build up, the same applies to people. *Talking* is the way to release the pressure! It becomes the valve to let the pressure go down slowly. How fast you release that pressure is up to you. Think of it as like a balloon – you can keep putting air pressure into the balloon, but eventually it will burst open.

Even if you are incredibly shy, if you recognize that, then talk to people about it. Everyone has suffered shyness for one reason or another, and even if you talk about the emotional stress you have, then you will find that it helps enormously.

There are also people who suffer what is classed as 'clinical depression' where they are in such a state of depression that they attempt self harm. The one thing to recognize is that you personally are not the only person that this has happened to.

It is also virtually impossible to help yourself, but there are people and organizations that can help you through it.

The brain is incredibly complex, and just as the body is affected by the different chemistry of foods that we eat, so too is the brain. Doctors have access to drugs that have been developed to treat depression, and there is nothing particularly sinister about them.

Just as diabetes is treated with insulin injections, so too can clinical depression be treated with drugs. There is no shame in this. It is simply logical. The main skill is recognizing that there is a problem, and then setting out to fix it.

With people who commit suicide, in most cases people around them have little or no idea that the person is suicidal.

There have been comedians who have committed suicide, and to the world at large they have looked like the happiest people alive. How could a person who is funny, be sad? Yet, in their private world, this has been very different, and they like everyone can suffer sadness and depression too!

It is also possible to be extremely lonely yet be surrounded by people!

While you may think that you are alone, and that no one loves you or cares about you, every single person is known to someone - and *someone*, in fact *everyone* feels sad when someone dies through suicide.

If you are feeling suicidal, don't be alone. Stay with people, talk, get involved in different activities, break your own normal routine, then change the things that are causing the pain.

If this means moving home or going to live in another city, or creating new group of friends, buying a dog, changing your university course or job, looking for a new boyfriend, taking up a cause, or becoming a volunteer, then do so. Do something about the problems you have. Don't think that the problems will solve themselves.

While death for any reason is sad, a suicidal death is one that people sense should not have happened. There is a general perception that it could have been prevented, and those left behind – brothers, sisters, parents, the friends have in some way let that person down, by not knowing, not understanding why it happened, and questioning what they themselves may have done to cause it.

The person who has committed suicide, does so to end their own pain, yet in so doing they create a huge pain, a great sense of loss and grief to *all* those around them. To a mother or father who loses a son or daughter, that loss will be with them forever. For them, as with any form of depression, their way out of their grief is through *time* and by *being busy, but the hurt will last a lifetime.*

Rarely do people who commit suicide think that their own death will affect other people, but it certainly will.

Certainly, there are grief counselors, just as there are psychiatrists and psycho analysts, and lots of other professional people to help. There are also various drugs to help people through depression, anxiety, and other problems, yet in a very human way the best, and most long-term solution is through your own *inner strength*, combined with *talking, time* and *being busy.*

Based on statistics, by far and away the greatest reason for youth suicide are relationship problems, followed by drug abuse.

After a suicide, most people who knew the person will be left wondering why it happened, and question why they didn't notice that something was wrong. Suicides mostly seem to come right out of the blue.

Carol was just sixteen, and to her friends she was completely normal. One day she simply stood in front of a train that killed her instantly. The train driver said she had a fixed look on her face as the train hit her. On board the train were all her school friends, who were devastated by what had occurred. Her whole family – brothers, sisters – older and younger cried for days, and the scar she left behind will probably never heal.

In the days following her death, the side of the train track became a mountain of flowers, but within a week they were all gone.

Would it have made a difference if she had talked with her parents, a doctor, or one of her teachers? We will never know.

Paul, also tried to commit suicide by throwing himself over a cliff. Instead of dying however, he broke his back, and now spends his time in a wheelchair. His life now is very different, and so too is that of his parents.

When a relationship breaks up, or one party rejects the other for whatever reason, it can be devastating to the other person. Being dumped, or rejected, or even abused or ridiculed when you thought the other person loved you, directly affects ego, pride, self esteem, confidence, drive, ambition and the list goes on. It can be devastating to the other party.

Relationships are built on trust, security, feelings, attitudes, commitment and ultimately love.

The break up of a relationship affects all of these emotional touch points, yet breakups are essentially a normal part of life.

As much as relationships bring out the best in people, they can also bring out the worst, and the rejected party may accept the breakup, sulk or alternatively become aggressive, depending on their personality type and the feelings they have at the time.

To get through a relationship breakup, or a huge argument, even the most devastating, it will take time, and again using the standard tools of staying busy, talking about how you feel and trying to break out of the depression through diverting your attention away from the immediate 'relationship problem' is the way to start feeling better.

Recognize that your relationship breakup or argument is just that, 'a relationship breakup' or 'argument'. Yes, it does affect you, just as it has everyone else who has been through one, and recognize that you are not the first person to experience a breakup and you won't be the last.

If you feel that this is the end of the world, you'll never find another person like her, and can only think about the other person, then your depression will grip onto you, and the longer this depression lasts, the harder it will be to break out of it.

Try to get your logic mind to take over from your emotions. Look to find something funny about your situation. Don't turn to alcohol if you intend purely to get drunk.

Alcohol can act to mellow the situation, but it may also heighten the problem if you use alcohol to punish or hurt yourself. The alcohol directly affects your reasoning skill, the skill you need most to get over the relationship breakup.

Almost one in three adolescents who commit suicide in the USA is intoxicated at the time they did it. Alcohol can well act as a depressant, so rather than making you feel good, it can have the opposite effect. If you are affected by alcohol in this way, don't have any, at least not until you are substantially over your immediate depression.

John was told the relationship was at an end and to 'get out'! He then had to leave the comfortable house that they had bought together and move to a friend's house. The room was small, the bed uncomfortable and then he discovered that the room was alive with fleas! How do you relate to a situation like this?

The easiest way is to laugh about the irony of the situation. Maybe the fleas had been thrown out of their love nests too! Afterall his partner had first thrown out the cat, next the dog, and now him! At least he was the last one to be thrown out!

Laughter can help ease the pain and help get you over or at least to some extent get over your depression.

Depression caused by a huge argument with someone, can be a mixture of depression and anger. Either way, they are both highly charged emotions.

When people get angry, they tend to want to hurt the other person, and given that they know you, they will aim their anger, where they know they will cause the most pain. People will often say things when they are angry, that they would never say under normal circumstances.

It is better to move away from the anger, than to react in anger too, but this is very hard. Anger is an emotional state, but people don't stay angry forever. Apologies often follow! Time to think about the reasons for the outburst is a great way of seeing the real issues, and solving them, without resorting to violence.

Depression caused through illicit drugs however is different. The drugs alter your perspective, distort the realities, and create delusions, mis- conceptions and anxieties. While different drugs will create different effects, illicit drugs are rarely a means of curing depression.

They may in fact cause depression, particularly when used a lot, and if you do have a drug problem, then this means getting help to break it. It also means that you, *yourself*, not someone else must want to break out of the drug cycle. This requires you to have the strength to do it.

There is so much to life, and the more you value your own life, and take pride in your achievements, the more likely you are to feel good about yourself and about life in general.

You will recover from a traumatic or bad relationship, forget about arguments you have, grow out of your self doubts, and find new things in life that will involve you. Just as your childhood was a stage of life, you are also going through a stage of life right now.

Definitely, our life will change and with each new stage of life you will find new challenges that confront you. With the right attitude you have the power within you to overcome any obstacle that is placed in front of you.

CHAPTER SIXTEEN
LOVE AND ALL THAT...

"The most important thing in life is to have the people who
love you around you for as long as you possibly can"

From the movie 'Sweet November' starring Keanu Reeves.

*A lot of people have difficulty defining where they call 'home'. It's very simple really.
It's the place where the people who care or love you the most are closest to you.*

How to start a relationship

High on the agenda of people, particularly in their teens and early twenties is the thought of
sex and romance.

Just like young puppies in spring, you will get excited by the chase, and all the possibilities of
what could be, will or won't happen. You will also be a bit scared about the possibilities too!

What if no-one wants to take you out, or you meet someone, but they are going out with
someone else?

Watching, waiting, admiring, planning, checking out others, wishing, hoping, getting involved,
going out to places on the hope of meeting someone special, getting jealous, staying involved,
getting dumped, dumping others, loving, hating, losing love and getting loved, feeling left out,
and being the center of attention – it's all in the game, and you can feel great one moment and
lousy the next!

When you were a little girl you probably thought that 'boys were yuk', and boys felt pretty much the same way about girls, but now the tide has turned. You probably can't wait to get involved with someone!

So, what can this book tell you that you don't already know?

You learnt all about sex in class at school. You know kids who "know all about it"; you've watched all the Soap Operas on TV, and heard kids brag about how fantastic they are!

You've also heard about condoms and aids as well as pregnancy, and a whole lot of things about what to do and what not to do. You've probably seen stuff on the internet, possibly watched R rated movies, and maybe even looked at the sex magazines in a newsagent, or at least seen how many sex magazines there are.

What you think about sex, love, boyfriends and girlfriends will have a lot to do with your values and the attitudes that you have developed over your lifetime.

Over the last few years your body has changed from that of a child to that of an adult. With girls, the physical changes happen at the beginning of puberty, whereas with boys they tend to happen at the end of puberty. That's why if you have a sister who is younger than you, she may have been taller than you for a year or so, and then you shot up!

What kicks in strongly in boys is what is called "androgens", the main one being testosterone, which are male sex hormones whose function is to produce secondary sexual characteristics after puberty, such as a deep voice and facial hair. Physically, testosterone causes physical changes a long time ahead of any emotional changes that take place. It is also the effects of testosterone that will also eventually make men go bald, but hopefully if you are a man you will have to wait a long time before this occurs!

Biologically, in both girls and boys there are a lot of complex hormonal changes taking place once puberty happens, and for the next few years after. It is during this period that our brains change to encompass 'a new reasoning power' to enable us to make complex decisions. Where as a child we saw issues as simply right and wrong, we start to see issues as an adult in more complex way, as our reasoning power starts to take effect.

Reading the results of Research surveys on youth, it would seem every girl and boy has experienced sex and drugs by the time they were fifteen! So, what do you think?

If you look at your friends and talk with them, is this really the case, or is it a case of the researchers being given 'spicy' answers, because this is what they want? Have you and your friends smoked marijuana on a regular basis, taken ecstasy, and been having sex for two or three years? If you read the newspapers or listen to news talk programs, you would certainly think that this is the reality, but what about your world? Is this the reality for you and the friends you mix with or someone else's world?

Using your new 'reasoning power' you will be able to isolate complex issues into rational thought; to see what is *seen* to be the truth, versus the reality of the truth; to decipher facts from conjecture; hype, hysteria and false motives as a basis for decisions. Your reasoning power is a powerful tool, and you need to use it well. The reality is what you see around you. That's your reality check. Not TV News.

Sure, we all want to seem more sophisticated and experienced than we are and be worldly wise, but while sex, drugs and violence are hot topics on TV, radio and in the newspapers, how close are they to the reality of your own life or the lives of your friends right now?

This is not to deny that sex, drugs and violence aren't happening. It is purely to say that, while these things do happen, it is still a minority of teenagers and not the majority who are involved.

If people are wishing to hype up an issue, they will rarely put the issue into context, or display all the facts. They may well highlight 2 or 3 facts, and simply ignore others that don't fit their argument. This is where your reasoning power comes in.

If you haven't been having sex and doing drugs, don't be sucked in to thinking everyone is doing this other than you! You are absolutely in the majority, and you have nothing to apologize for. You also don't need to make up your sex life or do something just because you think that is what is expected of you - just be yourself.

If you do want a relationship, and only if you do, then the most successful way of getting one is to put yourself in situations where you will meet people – people that you want to meet. You won't meet people by sitting at home watching TV by yourself, but you might if you invited some people over! You will also only meet people if you interact with them, and that involves talking.

While Prince Charming was 'very handsome', and Cinderella 'was very beautiful' on the night of the ball – not everyone will be handsome or beautiful, and even if they are, the most attractive quality will still be 'personality'. Even Cinderella had to go to the ball to meet someone special.

Personality wins hands down over looks every time – and it is this quality that will stay with you forever. It is also this quality that attracts others more than any other.

Think of Princess Diana. Was it her beauty, or her personality that captured the hearts of the world, making her 'the people's princess', 'the Queen of Hearts'?

Personality is not something that can be just switched on and off. There are no simple 'typecasts' of what the perfect personality is. Everyone is different, but in the love game, you may need to let your personality shine through more so than usual.

Remember when we talked about body language? Body language may be unspoken, but it is the first step in communication. You will react to body language, just as others relate to yours, even before you or they have spoken a word.

We all have what is called a 'body space' around us. This is the personal space around us, and we feel very uncomfortable if people break into this space.

You can go close to someone, but if you go too close, too soon, you end up invading their space, which can be very off-putting.

It is certainly easier to speak with someone with a smile, than it is to speak with someone who is staring blankly into space or appears to be angry. So, what's your body language saying now?

There are also times when it is OK to speak, and times when it is not. People will talk freely to other people at work or at college but would never dream of talking freely on a bus, train or in a lift.

For a long time, society has been ingrained the idea of "Stranger Danger" – the idea that if you don't know someone, then they could be a threat to you.

By ignoring the person, or otherwise avoiding eye contact you are supposed to be able to keep yourself safe. Talking should never be a crime.

On one hand avoiding eye contact or speaking is an individual protection device, but on a wider society level, it has conditioned people to stop talking. The silence on a bus or train, and the suspicions raised if someone does talk, are all to do with this society conditioning.

So, should you talk? If you want to get to know someone, you will have to, and you may have to even invent reasons to talk to 'break the ice'. The hardest part is getting up the courage to do so. It doesn't really matter what the conversations are about, be it the weather, a comment on the game you just watched, or it starts with an obvious line like "I haven't seen you here before. My name's John"! The main thing is to get a conversation going, so you better have your second line ready too! Once you have started a conversation, it usually becomes easier for a conversation to flow, but a conversation only works if it becomes two ways.

Some conversations will end up nowhere, and others will mean that you start to get to know more about the person you're talking to, or the first conversation may link you to other people.

The places you can start a conversation easily are usually when you are involved in something with other people – after sport, in a gym class, in a night class, at work in a break, at a lunch place, or pub after work. These are places where you have a reason to talk, won't feel threatened, and neither will the other person.

Joining a tennis club or charity or doing an evening course, flat sharing, and mixing with people at work will lead you to a wider circle of friends, and in turn put you in a place where you are more likely to meet people and potentially partners.

There are also on-line dating services too which can enable you to connect with other people on-line and if agreed to meet in person. If you do this, always meet first in a public space such as a restaurant not your home. While there are great people who use on-line dating services, you also need to be conscious of your own safety.

Getting to know a person and talking with people will also lead you into relationships.

If you ask around, you will find that most couples met through friends introducing them, on-line or through work or study, probably more so than through than going to pubs and discos. No matter where you meet, the first step towards a relationship is through talking.

Not everyone you talk to will be interesting, nor will you be interested in going out with someone just because they asked you! Through talking you will get to know if there is any empathy between you and the other person, and then you take it from there to share a meal, a movie, or simply spend time together.

CHAPTER SEVENTEEN
HOW FAR SHOULD YOU GO?

If you think getting a relationship is hard, keeping it is even harder!

Relationships are based for the most part on 'emotion'- on what you feel, and what the other person is feeling too.

They have feelings, just as you have feelings too. Maybe you want to know where the relationship is going, and the other person is wondering when it will end, or thinking about their last girlfriend, or 'horror of horrors' comparing you with her! Then there's the good friend who doesn't like you! What's his or her problem?

You may come away from a great night, with a promise from the other person "that they will call you tomorrow", only to find that they never call.

Perhaps you're not into the 'girlfriend-boyfriend' thing or they just wanted sex!

Like it or not, some relationships may last just part of a night, just one date, some for a week, others stop and start, and a few will stagger on for a year or two and get better or worse, or become a fairytale romance that lasts forever. There will be relationships that you are desperate to finish, while others you'll be desperate to cling onto!

There is simply no completely set way that relationships form, fall over or last. They will all be different, and while you may want certain things from your relationships, you may or may not get these things, and you may even change the way that you think as time goes by.

Being single gives you lots of freedom and you can have a lot of fun and great memorable times too, being free. There is absolutely nothing wrong with being single, just as there is nothing wrong with being married or in having a relationship.

Whatever your situation, you will probably receive pressure of some sort from someone, be it a parent or friends. What you do however is up to you.

A relationship starts initially with a conversation of some sort. If body language is positive and there is some rapport, there will be a lot of conversation and it will become obvious that the parties are interested in each other and want to see more of each other.

The body language may be subtle at first, but will develop through eye contact, and the intensity of the conversation and maybe smiles, laughs, facial expression and an occasional touch on the arm, shoulder, legs, feet or face, leading on to holding hands and gentle hugs and kisses. According to Researchers there are around 2000 different body language movements, so it will be hard to know which one you are picking up on but also if you are reading it correctly!

At each stage there will be checkpoints, to see if there is any resistance to what is being advanced. If there is no resistance then the process continues, however if there is resistance, then the advancing party will probably hold their position or withdraw slightly to ascertain whether there was really a lot of resistance, or it was slight, or just a play or tease.

This is all part of the love game. The process may be fast or slow. The two people may enjoy one date or progress to a series of dates as each person gets to know more about the other person.

Kisses may be a gentle kiss on the cheek, or a full lip kiss, or even a tongue kiss – and each gives a different signal to the one giving and the one receiving. A kiss on the cheek may mean "I like you"; on both cheeks may mean, "I studied French, and I'm very sophisticated! "or maybe," I don't know what side I like better!"; one on the lips, " I'm testing the waters"; a prolonged lip kiss may mean "I really like you a lot" or possibly " I think our relationship is getting hot"; and a tongue kiss means " I'm really wanting sex – where can we go?". A lot of words may be said, or none or maybe it will be a combination of body language and words.

Any of these kisses may be a total turn on, or a total turn off! They may give the right signals and get an equal response or give out absolutely the wrong signals and get total rejection. To give or receive a tongue kiss, or any other kiss at the wrong time, or in the wrong place could be the end of a relationship, even before it really gets started, so it is very important to read the body language correctly.

At a party, when everyone is dancing and having a great time, getting close to someone may be easier than trying to in the middle of a class. Timing is therefore critical.

Friday nights and Saturday nights have always been the "big nights" to go out. These days, and probably for the last fifty years, teenagers, as well as young adults go out on the Friday night, both male and female to have a great time and this may also involve drinking.

Drinking alcohol helps people to lose their inhibitions – their shyness, and the restraint they would normally have on the way they behave. No one can tell them what to do – no parents, no bosses, teachers or lecturers! They feel they can talk more, and are funnier, smarter, sexier and beautiful than they are normally, and they also feel they are more likely to either pick up or be picked up by the opposite sex.

The 'one-night stand' was born on a Friday night!

On the dance floor at a rave party with loud music and flashing lights or in a dark crowded bar, everyone looks great, and with the benefit of alcohol they look even better! Gorgeous guys, and beautiful women!

So, at the end of the night, you're invited to go home to his or her place, which just happens to be nearby, just for "a coffee or a drink".

"Sure, why not"! Your judgement here is most important as your own safety and well being is at stake.

One thing leads to another, and you find yourself in bed with him or her. Of course, you use a condom, and you have sex, but at five o'clock in the morning you wake up and look across at the person who you have just slept with and wonder how you ended up with this person. They look awful, as does the bedroom, so you quickly get your things together and get out of there, hoping they don't wake up.

Remember too, that the alcohol is still in your system, so if you're still drunk, walk or take a taxi!

When you get home, all you want to do is wash yourself as clean as possible and try and forget what happened last night. You don't even want to remember their name! You just hope they don't call, and that you didn't leave your phone number!

'One Night Stands' can be absolutely great, because they are unexpected or exciting at the time, or totally bad news!

You can have a totally great time and it can be the start of a new relationship. Equally, you may have a great time knowing that there won't be permanent relationship develop, because you or the other person are 'going away', which means that you don't have to show the normal restraints! You might also have a lousy time where you feel like a prostitute, feeling dirty because you've been with someone who you don't really know, and who you normally wouldn't want to be with.

Making a habit of having 'One Night Stands' will usually result in you feeling very depressed about the whole thing. While it might be exciting at the time, sex without feelings can be (but isn't always) an emotional vacuum.

For some people they look upon sex as a 'score board' of their own prowess. They don't want the commitment of a long-term relationship and may even find it more satisfying to be with one person tonight and someone else tomorrow.

Everyone is different, and their attitudes, beliefs, feelings will be either very similar to your own, or totally the reverse. They may also share their feelings or hide them away or simply use you. Being used by anyone is never a good feeling.

So, how do you develop a relationship that is more meaningful?

Very simply, it takes time, and it requires <u>both</u> people to feel the same way. Mention the word marriage, commitment or getting engaged and it could be the end of the relationship. While this may be your desire, the other person may be thinking more of their career first or going overseas or any of a hundred things before they want to settle down. They may also worry that the relationship is getting too intense and want out, way before it reaches that stage.

So, slow down a little. Take the time to get to know a person by doing different things together and apart. It's great to be together, but it's also great to be independent too. While there are certainly people who have married the first person they ever went out with, this is certainly not the case with most people, so live a little before you get too serious.

A girl saying, "I never want to get married and have kids", may mean that she really wants to. If she wears no rings on her fingers it may be a sign to say that she's available, and anxious to be asked out!

Similarly, a guy bragging about how he wants to stay single forever, may well be the first one to get married! The signals may all be very confusing.

Most people simply don't know what they want! Ask yourself if you have ever walked into a shop with no idea about what you want to buy, only to walk out with a shopping bag full of things you just purchased! It is much the same with relationships.

Both men and women as adults play games in relationships, not necessarily to deceive, often more for the excitement of it - to add mystery and desirability to themselves.

Relationships are based on a whole range of different emotional, physical and intellectual needs, and there is no single factor to determine why or why not relationships will or won't work.

Your feelings are the most important - how you feel and continue to feel during the relationship, both now and as time goes on.

At the start of the relationship, you may be well be totally excited by the 'new' love in your life. They seem totally exciting, beautiful and adorable, and you can't wait to see them again. Hopefully this feeling continues for a long time to come, but it may also go the other way as you start to see some of their individual faults, or traits of their personality or demeanor that bug you for whatever reason. This may be something simple like the way they sit at a table or eat, how they react to your friends, or the way they talk all about work.

The more you get to know a person, the more you learn about them. You will find out about what they like and dislike; about their friends and family; where they live now and where they have lived in the past.

Through conversation you will find out about the places they have traveled to and where they hope to travel to in the future; what they like in clothes, politics, music, films, fashion and food - a whole range of things that will either turn you on or turn you off. This is an exciting stage in all relationships, and it may well be that you find out things about your partner that very few other people will know.

The discovery phase may last a few dates or maybe a lifetime. Some people's past and conversation will bore you, and others you may find exciting, or even sad. Hopefully you will click together, but don't be totally upset if you don't. It's a pretty tall order to find someone you match with perfectly!

During this 'discovery phase' that you will either become more involved or less involved. You will also learn more in general about people and how they think, and many of the things you find out through relationships will probably surprise you or give you an insight into the way other people live in general.

In many ways we think that most people will be just like us, and when they are not, we can't work it out, or even work out why they think the way that they do. These differences are what make the world exciting.

Why do some people vote for the Democrats and others for the Republicans? Why are some people passionate about politics and others have no interest?

If everyone had perfect manners, brushed their hair the same way, had the same attitudes, wore the same clothes, we would find it pretty boring!

Being different doesn't mean that we must accept a person the way they are. They, but also you, may well change because of someone you meet. If the person loves water skiing, the chances are you will try it too, and learn through the experience. It is often more fun to say 'yes' than 'no'. Go ahead and try things that you haven't tried before. It may be as simple as eating a new type of food, parachuting out of a plane or hiring a boat together. Whatever it is, you might find you enjoy it.

There's probably nothing worse than going out with someone who doesn't want to do anything, so keep your mind open. You also need to respect the other person's feelings too, even when they don't want something that you really want to do. Don't however fall into the trap of becoming their servant or losing your self-respect. If you don't like something, say so!

Usually, it is much better to know that a person doesn't like something, rather than finding out second hand, or letting the 'problem' kill the relationship.

When people gossip or bitch about someone, they may never tell the person direct! This is part of the politics that underplay human behavior and especially relationships.

Relationships may be between two people, yet they also involve others, and others will impact on the relationship as well. Parents, friends, housemates, ex-girlfriends or boyfriends, workmates, old school friends are all part of the package.

So, how do you break up? Do you just drift apart, or simply not call, text or tell them on Facebook, or do you directly tell the other person that you want to break up? If your relationship is a long one, then breaking up will be a highly emotional time. It hurts if you are dumped, and it isn't much fun to tell someone that you want to break up either.

Break ups can and do occur, and there is no easy way to do it. There are relationships where you never want to see the person again (not easy if you work together or mix in the same social group), and there are softer relationship breakups, where you come to a mutual agreement that it is best that "you take a break from each other" or "just want to be friends".

There is a common statement that says - "treat others as you would like to be treated yourself". While it would be nice to live in a gentle world, people are emotional creatures. If someone says that "they love you" how do you reply? If you also love them, that's great, but if you were intending to break up, how then do you reply? Lying is not the answer.

Some true stories with names changed:

Story #1

James met Julia at a party. She had just arrived in the country from Germany and was living with her sister. The first month was great, and she asked if she could move in with him, which he agreed to. At first it was exciting but as time went on, James found himself inventing reasons why he had to stay at work longer and take a longer time to get home. His behavior had changed, and he subconsciously knew (his inner self) that they should break up. He told her, and they had a big argument, with James insisting that Julia move out to stay at her sister's place once again. Julia then phoned him a day later to say that she was pregnant. He was shocked and then he began to think about it. He didn't believe her, it seemed all too convenient, but what was he to do?

They talked it over and went to see a counselor and James continued to say that he didn't want to continue the relationship with her or have a baby. He would however pay for an abortion, which was only possible if she flew to another city. She agreed, and then flew off to have the abortion and then returned and met up with him again. She said that everything was fine, and that the abortion was done. Again, he didn't believe her, but took her at her word. And no, he didn't want to get back together.

A few months later James moved to the city where the abortion was to have taken place, (She was never pregnant) and then reading the afternoon paper he saw a picture of her, under the heading "German girl finds true love". The story related to an earlier story that the paper had run under the heading

"Poor little German girl just wants to find an American boy". James was stunned, and he was right, there had been no abortion, and no baby in the first place. She in turn had found her man, who was from the USA and subsequently she married him.

Story #2

Sacha met Peter at a nightclub and gave him her phone number to call which he did next day. They met for a date, and then continued to see each other for the next number of months. They became boyfriend and girlfriend, and Peter told her that he loved her and wanted her to marry her. She said no. Her previous boyfriend was returning from New York and while she had great feelings for Peter, she was really in love with her previous boyfriend. Peter was upset by this news but knew he couldn't change her mind. He had to move on, as much as it hurt. She did in fact marry the boyfriend from New York, but Peter rather than just walking away from the relationship and friendship they had built up, continued to be friends with both Sacha and the boyfriend/husband too.

Every relationship is different. No two are the same, and breakups do happen. There are those who want to break up and those who don't.

Breakups are certainly are not fun, can be charged with lots of emotional feeling, but they are also something that most people will experience in one way or another. Time heals all. Stay busy and know that you are not alone. That's what friends are for.

CHAPTER EIGHTEEN
SEX

The big issue.

Please don't read this chapter if you are offended by explicit language.

Having a statement like that at the beginning of this chapter may mean that this chapter is read more than others, but you should also respect others who will be offended by explicit language. To those people I apologize.

Like it or not we are all intrigued by sex, and while we do not like to talk about it, we do like to find out as much as possible about it.

Do you have a 'dirty mind', or are you just normal? Chances are you are much the same as everyone else.

Without doubt the most critical issue in all relationships is sex – where it happens, why it happens, how it happens, and with whom it happens are all important, and determine also how we feel.

Lots of sex, lack of sex, wishing for sex, avoiding sex, good sex, bad sex - sex has been a central feature in all relationships since time began. It can be the reason why relationships start, why they continue and why they finish!

So, why is sex so important? Traditionally, under church and family moral values, it was reserved purely for married couples.

These days with protection from pregnancy via the Pill, IUD's and condoms, it is possible to have 'protected' sex. Using a condom also helps avoid diseases like genital warts, Aids, Herpes, NSU, Syphilis, and Gonorrhea. Have 'unprotected sex' or 'unsafe sex' with someone you don't really know well is however very risky.

Having sex does not automatically mean that mutual love is involved, nor does it keep a relationship alive or guarantee that a relationship will continue to develop.

The legal age of consent varies from state to state. Maybe 16 or 18 but there is also nothing over that age to stop you legally from having consensual sex – consensual being the key word.

You could also refrain from having sex until after you are married, and there are still many people who will wait until after they are married before having sex. It's entirely up to you! You're the adult.

The general view, and probably right, is that when boys think about sex, they are very much focused on their own sexual organs – and the parts of a girl's body that they don't have – a girl's breasts and her vagina.

In contrast, girls are more likely to think about sex in a more romantic way. You have probably heard the expression, "A boy will give love to get sex, and a girl will give sex to get love!" Perhaps it's right, and perhaps it is wrong. Girls mature much earlier than boys do and are more likely to talk about sex in an intimate way with their girlfriends, than boys are with their male friends.

One thing is true, and that is that a relationship will never be sustained by sex alone! Girls will often complain that 'all that boys want is sex', and later "I gave him what he wanted (sex), and he dumped me!"

Just as having a baby will never sustain a marriage, or relationship, having sex to keep a relationship alive will also never work. There are men and women who are purely interested in sex and their own egos, and not in relationships, so don't assume that the feelings you have are the same for the other party.

Never be too easy! From a male perspective, a girl who is easy to pick up and sleep with will lose his respect. He may well sleep with her, but he won't want a relationship. Similarly, a man who sleeps around can also gain a reputation too.

There is a definite 'double standard' in society in relation to men sleeping around versus women. While men can largely get away with it, assuming they don't pick up a disease, "just sowing their wild oats", women are still labeled in the most derogatory terms as "she's easy" or worse still as a 'slut', 'whore' or 'the local bike'! Double standard or not, this is a reputation you don't want!

This doesn't mean that "all men are bastards"!

Just as there are good people and bad, there are good men in the world too, and there are more of them than there are bad. You simply need to find the right one.

It's easy to know if you are being sexually aroused physically. For boys, their penis starts to harden, while girl's nipples will stand more erect, and their vagina swells. These are the physical signs caused by blood flowing to these regions of the body, but there are also subtle changes in some people like eye colour changes and general body language communication.

While there are nice, sedate scientific words to describe sexual organs and sexual activity, the more common descriptions are more basic, and are often used as swear words. This happens in all languages, not just English.

On one hand we have romantic notions like 'making love', and 'hugs and kisses' while on the other hand we have guttural terms like 'getting fucked', and the list goes on.

Sex can be very basic and animalistic, and both men and women can be sexually aroused 'being basic' or 'talking dirty' just as much as they can be by being 'romantic and passionate'. Both styles of language have their place, but don't mix the two up!!

The reason there are so many R rated movies, porn sites and magazines is a lot to do with these guttural urges and stimulating the sexual desires of the viewer or reader. In a similar way, romance novels, magazines and films also stimulate the idea of 'romance', all designed to stimulate the viewer's desires or imagination, and increasing the sexual urge.

While some people will find it easy to 'talk dirty', other people will be highly offended by this sort of talk. People are all very different.

Great sex happens when you really feel good about each other, and really work hard to make your partner feel good as well as yourself. Sex is about feeling and touching, stimulation and arousal. It works on both the body and the mind, and the lead up, or 'chase' can be just as much fun as the sex itself.

People have had sex in a million strange places, anywhere from the top of a mountain to a park bench, underwater and in the air. The most usual place however is in a bed! Sex can be very spontaneous, or planned, but when it is spontaneous, it is most likely going to happen in an odd place, and again this adds to the excitement!

Like a game of hide and seek, sexual play is a balance between being 'naughty' and 'nice' and we all have the 'naughty' and 'nice' sides to our personality! This is all part of the excitement, the lead up - the sexual gameplay! These games are all important parts of the overall 'sexual game', and if you leave this gameplay out, then the chances are that the 'sex' will be more functional (boring) and less driven by emotion (exciting/fun).

Sex can last a minute or for hours. You have heard the expression, 'just a quickie', and 'wham, bang, thank you ma'am', to describe sex that is over in a few minutes, and you have also heard about sex that lasted all night long, expressed in a boastful way like 'we fucked our brains out' or 'we fucked ourselves stupid' or in nice terms like "I'm so in love", and "we had such a g-o-o-d weekend!"

The times however when you are relaxed, feeling good, are with someone you really care about, and in a place where you feel good too, are the times that you will remember as the best times. These times will become your warm and fuzzy memories.

As much as we relate 'emotionally' to another person, we also relate 'physically'.

While this physical attraction will differ from one person to another – some people are tall, others short, fat, thin, blonds, brunettes and the list goes on – the fact remains that physical attraction is an important part of the sexual equation. We can be 'physically attracted', 'physically indifferent' or 'physically repulsed'.

Having sex with someone means that we will be getting very, very close to them, not just admiring someone in the distance or on TV.

We will be physically touching their skin, their hair, lips and body, and they will be touching yours, putting their own body, hands, fingers and sexual organs into us or over us! We will be able to explore their body, touching, feeling and caressing their body in all its nakedness, and they will be doing the same to yours.

We therefore need to feel comfortable doing this! If we don't want to touch them, or have them touch us, then if we do go ahead, we will not feel good about the sex, or ourselves.

If you are 'emotionally' and 'physically' attracted to another person and their body, then there is nothing more exciting then the feel of their body next to yours. Their skin will have a textural feeling to your touch, and probably a perfume or smell, coming from their body oils and the shampoo or perfumes they use. Their hair may be soft, and their body smooth and curvaceous. Whatever it is, it will have a distinct quality to it, and it will be different to our own.

To feel and touch someone's body and let them touch us is a very intimate moment. We have always showered and undressed ourselves throughout our lifetime, we now have another person also seeing and touching us too. This can be an exciting moment, or one that also causes stress.

Undressing each other, having your partner unclip your bra, remove your panties, and you unbutton his shirt and take his trousers off are all part of the sexual play, heightening sexual desires and expectations.

To shower together, rubbing each other's body with soap and water, and kissing, holding and massaging each other's bodies all over, before drying each other off, again heightens the sexual desire and becomes part of the foreplay. It is a way of showing how you care, how you feel, and making yourself feel good about your partner as well as yourself. You may even make love in the shower!

Showering and undressing your partner like this not only build you and your partner's sexual desires and expectations, but it also extends the sexual play, adding a touch of romance and fantasy to the pleasure of the moment.

Just as we tease each other verbally, we can also tease each other with our bodies. We may know that we want sex. Our bodies are telling us this, yet we are playing hard to get! Giving yet taking.

There is nothing wrong with this.

The more that this game can be extended, the more sexually aroused we become.

While we can certainly jump ahead in the game, we can also go out of our way to 'play'.

The more feeling, touching, caressing, kissing, fondling, hugging and foreplay we have the more sexually aroused we become.

There is also an element of the 'warrior' and the 'princess', the image of the strong powerful warrior hardened by battle, coming to rescue the princess alone in her castle! The vanquished and the conqueror! The powerful and the weak! The lion chasing the gazelle!

While these images are stereotypes, they remain as images within a fairytale romance, part of our own 'sexual fantasy', all be it played out in a hundred different ways, or as a role reversal where the woman plays the dominant role.

By all that we say and do, we communicate our feelings, and we can be either great lovers or lousy ones!

We may talk a lot, or not at all, but any compliments we give should aim to bring pleasure. If you like what you're doing say so; if you love her body, or think he has a great body, say so. We all respond to compliments.

When it comes to position, there are as many as your imagination can handle! If a penis can enter a vagina, and a rhythmic back and forward action occur, then sex can happen!

You can make love front to front, side to side, front to back, straddled on the side of the bed, in the bed, on the bed, beside the bed, against the wall, on the floor, sitting, kneeling, in a yoga position or with one partner taking up one position and the other another.

You can be head-to-head, spread eagled or tightly held, legs wrapped around each other, on top, or below. This may of course depend on how fit or adventurous the two of you are!

A friend of mine rented a hotel room for he and his girlfriend which only had two single beds connected as one. Feeling like superman, he did a great leap into bed, but the beds parted company and he fell to the floor breaking his leg. So much for the Romantic weekend

We could be fully naked; just in our underclothes, dressed or dressed up! We can make love under the sheets, or on top of them, and you could have sex in the bedroom, the bathroom, the car or any place else in the house or outside at any time of day. There are simply no fixed rules!

There is one rule that you should never cross. If the other party says 'No' or is not willing to go further, you need to respect that decision – No means No.

Where a lot of relationships eventually fail is when sex starts to take on a routine – only in bed, only on a Friday night just before falling asleep, all in the same position as last week, timed to the minute and so on.

Sex is just one part of a relationship.

Just as each of us have different looks, we also have different sexual organs too! Not every man will have a huge penis – it may be long, fat, thin, circumcised or not, and every woman will be different too! While some girls will have a very tight vagina, others will have a wide one, and it may be very dry or instantly wet. If it is very dry, and doesn't moisten easily, it may be necessary to use KY Jelly or Vaseline to make it easier for the penis to enter. There is nothing wrong in doing this. What you are looking for is for the penis to easily go in and slide over the surface of the vagina without pain or hurting.

Sex that is painful is not fun. It is the friction on the sides, and tip of the penis, and at the sides and top of the vagina as the penis slides back and forward that creates the pleasure. What we are feeling is a series of spontaneous muscular contractions that we feel as intensely pleasurable erotic sensations. These sensations will lead to a climax, orgasm or orgasms in a woman and to ejaculation in a man when a series of sperm are spurted through the head of his penis into the woman's vagina, or into the end of the condom.

While a woman may not experience any orgasm, she may well have one or a whole series or orgasms. The man however will in general only be able to sustain one ejaculation before the erection falls away.

A second or sustained erection may be possible after a few minutes of extra excitement, and a second ejaculation follow soon after or a little later in the night.

Unfortunately, following ejaculation, there is a natural tendency for men to want to sleep. The woman may well be still in the mood!

The absolute best sex is when the man and the woman both 'come' at the same time!

The greatest criticism of men is that they 'came too soon', and from men that they wished 'that women would come faster!'

While there are no guarantees that this will be possible, the surest way to ensure that the woman achieves an orgasm is to stimulate the clitoris, 'the magic button', just above the opening to the vagina, before sex and during it. The magic button becomes erect as sexual stimulation occurs, and the area around it, the vulva, is sensitive too, and can also be stimulated! This stimulation may be done with a finger, either the male or female, or by massaging the clitoris with the tip of the penis, or even by using your tongue. Some women and men like this and others hate it – so be sensitive to your partner's wishes.

Some women will like this stimulation or masturbation to be done very slowly, while others like it to be like a rapid agitation of the area. It may also be done while the penis is moving back and forward in the vagina, so that the woman is receiving stimulation both inside the vagina, and around the clitoris at the same time. This greatly improves the chances of a woman achieving an orgasm.

Some women like the movement of the penis to be slow, gentle and rhythmic, while others like it to be rapid and deep, or have a variation in pace and position.

When the penis is first to enter the vagina, if only the tip is entered and it is thrust back and forward at this length, before being thrust to its full length the whole way in, this can also build the sexual pleasure for both of you. This is all part of the tease, the sexual play.

There is also no reason why the penis must stay always inside the vagina throughout sex. It may enter once, or may be withdrawn at different times, and the vagina stimulated by use of a finger or fingers, with the erect penis reinserted as and when desired. Hopefully this will give the woman more time to achieve an orgasm, and slow down the man's ejaculation.

While the 'penis' and 'vagina' are central figures in the sexual play, they are not the only players! What you do with your hands, lips and body are critical too! The more you use these other parts of your body, to caress, fondle, grope, kiss, hold and touch the better.

The one on top can rest all their weight on the other person, or none of it.

His hand can run through her hair, or fondle her breasts, teasing her nipples, or her hand can play with his ears, hold onto his balls, or grip his buttocks. The body can be supported by the other body overall or all its weight pivoted on his penis – a real high-flying act! The more times that you have sex, the more likely you are to find out what your partner likes and what they don't!

Ideally the man should try to hold their ejaculation until after the woman has achieved her orgasm, but this may happen sometimes and sometimes not.

Everyone wants to hold on to the feeling, the pleasure that it gives!

While good sex should give lots of pleasure for both parties, it doesn't always follow that all sex is good. It is possible to have bad sex, all be it with the right or wrong partner and to be disappointed, sad, or wistful. If this does happen, you need to think carefully about why it happened this way, and to do something about it.

Remember your inner and outer self that we talked about in an earlier chapter?

After sex, it is also a good habit to wash your vagina, or penis, and ideally to urinate as well. While this is not a complete safeguard against sexually transmitted diseases, it may help wash or flush any nasties away. It's simply good hygiene!

As to oral sex, it also comes down to you - how you feel. The same emotional, physical, morality, and hygiene issues apply even more strongly in relation to oral and anal sex than they do in conventional sex.

There may be partners who you would be happy to have oral sex with, and ones that you would never want to. Never do something you don't want to do.

Most people are attracted to the opposite sex but there are people too who are happy to sleep with anyone of the same or opposite sex. There are also men and women who are attracted to their own sex only. You should be aware of this and realize that they will not necessarily tell you everything about themselves, particularly if there are things about their sexual behavior that they don't want you to know.

Having sex with someone does not mean that they were not having sex with someone else last night. If they were, how likely is it that they will tell you? Even people with Aids have been known to lie about it and infect others. Not everyone has your values.

It should be a rule not to have sex without some protection, particularly in the early part of a relationship. Unprotected sex could result in a pregnancy and that will change your life or give you herpes or other disease.

There are many girls who have had a child when they are in their teens, and that will also involve the dad too – in child support or other financial or emotional ways. As a parent, no matter what your age, that is a huge responsibility, and if you are not ready or had other plans for your life, then the new baby will change that forever. There is however no greater love than that of a parent for their child, and if you do get pregnant or your girlfriend becomes pregnant, then you need to talk about it a lot, and make decisions early both for yourselves and for the unborn child. This is a big decision point and will have an enormous effect on your life and that of your child and partner.

Today being a lesbian or homosexual is no longer the 'sin' that it was once considered. Gay rights, coming out, gay pride, the Gay community have all helped break down traditional prejudices in most societies.

Many countries have legalized same sex marriage, including Australia, Canada, France, Germany, South Africa and around twenty other countries.

This doesn't mean that it is easy to be gay. There are still many prejudices that exist and the 'emotional roller coaster' inherent in all relationships is just as prevalent in gay relationships as it is in heterosexual ones.

Just being homosexual or a lesbian does not mean that you will be attracted to all lesbians or all homosexuals!

The difficulties of finding the right relationships are just as hard for gay couples as they are for heterosexuals if not more so, and as individuals, gay people have the same moral, emotional and physical issues to contend with as everyone else.

In today's world there are people who have always been gay, and there are people who have been married and had kids, only to leave a marriage and take on a gay relationship.

There are also people who were gay, who have gone straight, and straight people who have become gay.

Having friends who are gay, or who are straight, does not mean that it necessarily follows, that you are or will be either gay or straight. Through all of this you will determine your own path.

No matter what, you must be true to yourself, more than anyone else.

CHAPTER NINETEEN
FOOD

Learning to cook as well as eat!

Let's face it, over the last number of years you have had your fair share of McDonalds and other fast food, and probably you love chips, hamburgers, chocolate and anything that is fast to get and fast to eat. It's easy to buy food like this but also hard to avoid it!

Most of the foods we like have too much sugar and fats in them. We also know that there are 'good' foods, but because they don't have the sugar, fats and salts that the junk food has, we can find them boring.

No doubt your mother has told you lots of times to eat an apple, eat your vegetables, drink water and not a soda, and of course you know she is right, but will you follow her advice?

As an adult your taste buds will change! Up until now, you have probably avoided trying new types of food, on the basis that 'you don't like it', and you could be as fussy as you liked, given that someone else, probably your mother was doing the cooking!

As an adult you are in charge of what you eat and have a choice. You could simply buy junk food or broaden out your food horizons to include new foods that you haven't tried before. There are so many choices around. You can also start doing your own cooking!

If you know how to cook, that's fantastic, but if you don't, then maybe you should learn!

Like anything else, cooking is a matter of learning some fundamentals, and then by trial and error, you learn through experience.

You also need to approach cooking with the right attitude. Think positive, and don't be embarrassed if you stuff it up. It's easy to burn food, overcook it, undercook it, leave out vital ingredients, or put the wrong ones in – but don't worry - you will learn what works and what doesn't, even if you do get beaten up by your housemate for ruining his or her best saucepan!

Just like learning to swim, you must get in the water, not just read about how to swim.

So how do you cook, or learn to cook?

The main ingredients used for cooking are pretty much universal.

There are a whole lot of different meats – beef, lamb, pork, and lots of exotic ones like venison, and so on; different poultry types – chicken, duck…. and lots of different types of seafood, which vary from place to place around the world. There are also alternatives to animal meats too.

Then there are all sorts of vegetables, spices and products made from, or derived from different food combinations, as well as a number of grains like rice and wheat, which may be grains in their own right or processed into other forms – like wheat into pastas, or corn into oil, flour or other product.

From seaweed to mushrooms, bones to broccoli, squid to sauces, there is an incredible array of food available for people to eat.

Certain foods are identified with certain cultures – rice and noodles with the Chinese, hamburgers with Americans, curry with Indians, spaghetti with Italians, potatoes with Irish, and beef with Argentineans, but these days all these foods have moved globally and been incorporated into the food diets of people around the world.

As much as people enjoy Fast Food, there is now a movement evolving into 'Slow Food', food that is savored for its taste sensations, preparation skill and presentation.

It is now possible to see Bulgarian cheese, South African wine, to buy Swedish roll mops, Moroccan cous-cous, Malaysian Sambal, Jamaican coffee and Canadian tuna in supermarkets around the world. As our taste buds have expanded to take on new flavors, new ingredients and new products have created an exciting world of food possibilities.

With all these fantastic ingredients available, where do you start?

While it may be possible to instantly try to cook a gourmet meal for six, the chances are this may be a little ambitious, though not impossible! It is far easier to start with something less ambitious.

While food is all about taste, it is also a lot to do with presentation, and the sharing of food with others, through the conversation and atmosphere that is created.

If we look at breakfast, we can just 'grab and run', or we can sit down formally at a table, and have a leisurely breakfast eating, talking, and maybe reading the morning paper.

Coffee or tea can be prepared as instant coffee, using tea bags, or tea brewed and presented in a pot. All may be acceptable, but one has more style, taste and through its presentation creates an atmosphere for the table as a whole.

Toast can be made from all sorts of breads, and can be presented in a toast rack; jams and butter presented in their own special dishes, or just as the jar from the shop, similarly juices in a jug, or just from the bottle, or freshly squeezed?

That little extra trouble in preparation and in presentation will add enormously to the sense that the food looks better and tastes better too.

Bacon and eggs – cooked slowly, not fast on a medium heat, and presented on a warmed not cold plate, with gently fried hot mushrooms, and hot quarters of tomato, can be a treat. The art is in the cooking and the presentation. If the egg is smashed, with the bacon burnt, or semi cold, and the tomatoes greasy, then the look and taste of the breakfast is just not the same. Cooking bacon and eggs, or pancakes for breakfast, and making the effort to present breakfast in a stylish way, is a great way to start learning how to cook.

Having conquered breakfast and decided that you want to move on to bigger things, the same rules apply. Look to making a nice presentation as well as doing a good job at cooking.

Start by buying some recipe books, and simply reading what goes into different dishes. There are fantastic recipe books available, on all sorts of cooking styles – and the more you use them the more you will learn the techniques involved in cooking good food.

A lot of people never use recipe books, thinking that in some way, either they know better, or that they couldn't be bothered, but recipe books are like guide books on how to do things, and the combinations of ingredients have all been trialed before being written, so your cooking becomes less of an experiment.

When you find a recipe that you like and find that it is easy to cook with great results, mark it with your comments for use again in the future.

Once you learn to cook just a few dishes that you like to eat, then you are well on your way to becoming a cook.

Things like spaghetti are easy to cook, but there are ways of making it taste good and ways to make it taste bad. The same thing applies to rice. Every country in Asia likes their rice cooked in slightly different way, and if you can learn to cook it in a few different ways, it will become more interesting to eat. It might be that you even buy a Rice Cooker, and use the Rice Cooker to prepare the rice each time you cook, but then you could add saffron to make it yellow, buy a different type of Rice like Basmati or Saffron rice, adding an egg or chopped vegetables to it to create a different taste and presentation.

By having a few ways of preparing the rice, or different types of Pasta, or potatoes (boiled, steamed, French style, chipped, whipped, baked, foil wrapped etc), you will be creating a whole repertoire of accompaniments for your main meal.

The same thing applies to salad. Having a whole range of ways to present salads, means that you can pre-prepare a meal ahead of time and if the salads taste great, then the main meat, poultry or fish will also then become easier to prepare, because you have the side dishes under control.

You then don't need to stress out trying to cook a whole lot of dishes together at the same time – running out of bench or oven space or creating a massive clean up of dishes after the meal.

For an Indian Curry, you might prepare a range of small salads – chopped green apple and natural yoghurt with sultanas; banana with coconut; chopped tomato and white onions in white vinegar; and chopped cucumber in vinegar, and some chutneys in their own small dishes. All of these are easy to do, and it means that you can relax, and concentrate on preparing your curry or curries.

Salads to go with a bar-b-cue can be totally different – potato salads, green salads, pasta salads, Greek salads - the list is endless. The more interesting the salads, the easier it is to make the main meal come together. With most vegetables there are many varieties of the same type.

There are different varieties of lettuce, potatoes, cucumber, and the list goes on, so it is also easy to experiment using these different varieties.

If you are cooking steak on a grill or bar-b-cue, the trick is to start with a hot plate not a cold one, and then cook it on one side only until the juices come through. Only then do you turn it over, to seal these juices in.

There is a general tendency, when you first learn to cook, to put the stove on full heat whenever you cook something, thinking that in this way, the cooking will happen faster. This is usually wrong. It simply means that you will more than likely burn or dry out whatever is being cooked or cook the outside and not the inside. Using a recipe book will help guide you towards the right level of heat as will experience.

A stove may be gas or electric or even burn wood, and will usually have an oven, a grill and various hot plates with different size plates. You then have different types of saucepans, frying pans, and maybe even a wok. These are great for cooking with, because all the juices flow to the centre, and you are less likely to burn things as you go.

When you put ingredients together, you will find that each has a different cooking time. This means that you have to think out the timing of each of the dishes you are cooking, so that they all arrive at the same 'ready to eat' time. It will really spoil the meal if the carrots are overcooked, and the meat semi raw!

If you intend to use a recipe, pre plan it by buying the ingredients well ahead of time.

That way if there is something that is out of season, or hard to find, you will have a little extra time to find it or an alternative.

Just because a recipe calls for lots of different types of ingredients, doesn't mean that it is hard work. The more ingredients, the more taste sensations that are created, and while a recipe may call for lots of ingredients, often these are combined at various stages into sauces or blends of spices to use, so while it may look like a lot of work, it may in fact be easy.

There are also cooking classes organized by evening colleges for amateur cooks to go to. These can be good fun, and you not only get to try different foods, but also get to meet other people too.

With so many food courts, fast food, delivery services and restaurants around it is relatively easy to avoid cooking altogether, and simply rely on others to do the cooking for you.

I recently heard of a new kitchen being put into a house, which simply had a bench and two dishwashers. The bench was for opening the take away dishes, and the two dishwashers were there so that the dishes could be moved from one to the other! No need for a stove at all!

It really doesn't matter whether you are male or female, cooking can be fun, and it is a great skill to have, not just so that you can cook for yourself, but also so that you can cook for others. Give it a go. You might find that you like it.

It doesn't matter if you have a great job, or are unemployed, if you have the skill to cook, you will always be in demand. Food is a big part in all our lives and being able to cook a nice meal and share that with others is a skill that will serve you well throughout your whole lifetime.

CHAPTER TWENTY
HOW GOOD AN ADULT WILL YOU BE?

As much as this book can give you an insight into life as an adult and some of the issues you may face, there is no substitute for living and the experience you will gain.

A book can never cover every issue that you will face in life, nor give you the answers to all the questions that you may ultimately have.

Hopefully this book has however given you some understanding into what life as an adult is all about, how you can plan your life ahead, and maybe avoid some of the pitfalls.

The fact that you have read this book, means that you are thinking about life in general, and particularly about your own life and what lies ahead.

Most people don't have any plan in their life. They simply move through life, knocked over and picked up by events and circumstances that confront them. They let life control them, rather than them controlling life. By understanding how the adult world works, you have a better insight into how people think, and how you will be able to cope with the twists and turns, and ups and downs that occur.

Problems will occur in your life, just as they do in everyone's life, but for every problem that arises, there is also a solution – be it a good solution or even a bad one.

If you make mistakes, recognize them, and do something about them. Don't hide away from them. Talk about them. The more you talk, the more you find that the problems and mistakes you make can be overcome.

Don't let problems knock you down. Get up and try again. Everyone gets kicked, but they also can kick back too!

The Chinese say that whenever you have bad luck, you must 'counter' that bad luck by doing another deal. If you miss out on a job, or a date, a study course or buying something, immediately go for another – to 'counter' the luck.

You will never starve if you still have your hands to work with and a brain that can work things out. Look after them and they will look after you.

Also do a little of what former President of the USA, John F. Kennedy said "Do not ask what the country can do for you, ask what you can do for your country".

It is always better to give then receive.

CHAPTER TWENTY-ONE
GO FOR IT

Everyone has a different view on life, and often people have a special viewpoint on how they live their life.

Here are some of them.

Jeff, a printer, aged 40 was married when he was 22, and now has 3 children. He has just purchased a new printing press for $3 million, with a seven year long lease on the equipment and a three year lease on new premises. He will be borrowing virtually every dollar.

If the business succeeds, he should be well off. If it fails, he will lose everything, including his house. What drives him?

He says - "It's the fire in my belly… the sense of achievement". So how important is money? Jeff "knows it's a necessity. It's a vehicle to get the lifestyle".

So, what was he doing when he was 18? He says "I was an average student. I just couldn't apply myself to study. Deep down I wanted to be a doctor, but I couldn't write essays. At 18, for me it was mass confusion. I didn't know where to go, but I got on well with people, and then a job came up which got me into sales.

Why did he get married so young? "It seemed to be what all my friends were doing".

His advice to an eughteen year old is "be prepared to change direction at any time, and learn from as many people as you can. Make yourself streetwise. Don't just go down one path".

Talking about himself in the third person he says: "he will never die saying what if'."

....

"Ability can be assessed fairly accurately by a person's academic record and achievement in work. Character is not so easily measured. After some successes and too many failures, I concluded that it was more important, though more difficult to assess a person's character"

Lee Kuan Yew
Former Prime Minister of Singapore

....

Michael aged 27 was married when he was 24, with his wife expecting their first child in a few weeks time. He grew up in Dublin in Ireland and is 1 of 3 brothers. Although he is working in Accountancy, he is still not sure what career path he wants to take.

At 18 he was living at home and thought he would be a millionaire by the age of 30. It never crossed his mind to leave home. He was very happy there.

Nine of his friends however decided to go to Australia for a year. After speaking with his brothers, dad and boss, and then ignoring all of their advice, Michael and his 9 friends left for Australia.

All his mates have now returned to Ireland... one who couldn't get a job and only lasted 4 months in Australia, has since won the Irish Lottery and is now a multi millionaire.

Michael's biggest regret is that he didn't do his professional exams, and his advice to others is "no matter how difficult it seems, try to get a formal education."

Life he says gets more serious as you get older, but "don't forget to enjoy life". He also recommends traveling for a year – especially Ireland!

....

"What is stupid is to pretend you are smart. When you pretend to be smart, you are at the height of stupidity"

"Live a little. Do something daring and a little risky every day. This habit will keep your life exciting and keep you younger for years longer"

"Sight is what you see with your eyes. Vision is what you see with your mind".

Robert Kiyosaki
Author of 'Rich Dad Poor Dad' books

Chandon, aged 39 grew up in a village in Fiji, before moving to New Zealand to go to a bigger school at age 16. He had always liked science because that's what people who did well, did".

His dream was to become a Pharmacist. Seeing the lifestyles in New Zealand made him realize that "you could be whatever you wanted to be". It also forced him into the realization that he didn't want to do Pharmacy, and even though he gained admission to pharmacy at University in New Zealand, he decided he wanted to do Arts and Finance. His family was devastated! All his friends were doing Medicine, and he had to return to Fiji and face his parents, and the "stigma" of having failed by not going into Pharmacy or Medicine.

He completed his degree in Finance in Fiji before joining a Bank there. Within a year, he was heading the Marketing, Advertising and Promotion Department, and loving the job.

He then decided to give his job up and move to the United States with his wife and two children to an unknown future. He had decided that the politics in Fiji, and the racial tensions that were building up between indigenous Fijians and those of Indian decent, made his future in Fiji uncertain, and with his wife and two children, he moved to Los Angeles. His first job was sweeping the floors in a warehouse, a job he did for 3 months, before moving into Administration, and later Banking.

It took many years to get his family back on side, after his shock decision not to do Pharmacy. Today he loves what he is doing as a Small Business Manager with the bank. He has also continued his study, completing a Finance Degree and in his spare time he has developed an interest in Oil Painting and sketching. Chandon is also actively involved in community projects, helping to raise funds to educate the children of poor Fijian Indian Farmers.

A Background Note: The Indian Fijians originally were brought to Fiji by the English to work in the sugar plantations. When they finished their indenture, they had a choice of paying for a return ticket to India or being given a 99 year long lease on land which they could work themselves. Most took up a lease, but when Fiji received its independence in 1970, these 99 year long leases were reduced to 30 years, and now today the leases are running out and are not being renewed by the indigenous Fijian owners. The Indian population who have all been born in Fiji, have lost their land, and now face an uncertain future.

Chandon's advice to a 18 year old – "Stretch your resources to the maximum. Don't just go with the flow". In-spite of his own background, he also says "that there is still a lot of value in traditional values… don't reject them, simply because they are traditional".

……………………………..

"If I had known I was going to last this long I would have taken better care of myself"

Christina Cock
Who died in 2002, aged 114

"The best way to live, is to be there for other people…"

Charity Organizer

"Touch is the greatest healer of all"

Acupuncturist

"If you think you are too small to make a difference, just spend a night in a dark room with a mosquito…"

Margaret Fulton, renowned Cookbook writer

"Everyone of us should think high of ourselves, no matter how low we may be. The only way to come up from low is to think high…If you don't think positive the negative takes over".

Rev. Solomon Burke, Los Angeles minister and soul singer

……………………………….

Glenn wanted to become a 'Museum Curator', because he had an interest in animals and natural history. He never has.

He did however complete a Zoology degree, and then continue to work for the University doing research on Mosquitoes and Malaria, a project funded by the World Health Organization, before transferring to the University's Entomology Department in charge of their insect breeding colony.

He then spent the next 15 years working for a government research organization as a Research Scientist. Having bought an old house, which was classified by the National Trust, Glenn became interested in Antiques and restorations. His father had been a French Polisher by trade.

This led to him setting up his own Antique shop, and he has run the shop very successfully for a number of years. As he says, "if you can make your hobby your profession, what more could you want?"

His biggest frustration in life was not being able to help his wife when she was dying from cancer. Despite his scientific background, all he could do was to be there.

Glenn works by his own moral code – this being honesty, compassion and thoughtfulness. He feels that if you follow your own moral code, then the universe will look after you. Money, he says, can be made anywhere. Just sit down and think of something that is really useful to someone".

"Thick skin? Thin Skin? How tough should you be? Keep calling! Who will break first?"

His advice – "don't be like a lot of people and put aside your dreams…if God's given you a talent, use it".

He also recommends that everyone should have a total physical Health check each year, including a blood test. With so many pollutants in the air, and food additives, the earlier you detect a problem, the easier it is to fix. If you want to do this cheaply, give blood each year. It helps other people, and they will notify you if there is anything wrong".

And his final advice – "Live for the day you're in, don't plan too far ahead, because you don't know what will happen."

……………………………..

"Money is like an arm or a leg; use it or lose it"

Henry Ford
Founder of the Ford Motor Company

"… Don't rest on your laurels, and take nothing for granted"

Film Director and actor Ron Howard
Actor in 'Happy Days', and now one of Hollywood's foremost movie directors.

....

"It is the mind that makes the body rich. There is no class so pitiably wretched as that which possesses money and nothing else"

Andrew Carnegie (1835 -1919) who left his 350 million dollar fortune to foundations and charities

....

"Laws are like sausages. It is better not to see them made"

"Never believe in anything, until it has been officially denied"

Otto von Bismarck, German Chancellor in 1870

"What we do during our working hours determines what we have; What we do in our leisure hours determines what we are".

George Eastman(1854-1932)
Founder of Kodak

Buddhists have six virtues that they strive for – generosity, honesty, joyous effort, patience, concentration and wisdom. None of these are easy to obtain.

....

The definition of insanity is doing exactly the same as you are doing now and expecting a different outcome.

....

"I love to see what people do with their hands and their imagination"

Entertainer
Michael Jackson

....

"I've never met anyone who has forgotten where they have come from…I've met people who run from where they have come from, but none that ever forgot"

Bruce Springsteen
"The Boss"
Singer/entertainer

"Here, there's no difference between the rich and the poor, just the happy and the miserable"

Brazilian Bar-owner

Now, it's your turn!

Read the book, write down whatever you want to, and when you are ready pass the book on to someone who you think will appreciate it, or recommend it to a friend.

Who knows what or where this book will travel to or the life that you will lead!

Just like this book, there is no clear path as to where you or this book will be read this year or in the years to follow...

Books like this one are launched like a ship, and then they travel beyond via the internet in journeys as diverse as life itself.

I hope you have enjoyed reading this book.

Welcome to the adult world.

Good luck and have a great life.

Geoff Stuart
Author